30 GAMES
FOR
SOCIAL CHANGE
CRITICAL THINKING FOR ESL/EFL CLASSES

JANINE BERGER

WAYZGOOSE PRESS

30 Games for Social Change: Critical Thinking for ESL/EFL Classes

Copyright © 2016 by Janine Berger

Edited by Maggie Sokolik.

Book design by DJ Rogers.

Published in the United States by Wayzgoose Press.

ISBN-10: 1-938757-28-9

ISBN-13: 978-1-938757-28-0

Table of Contents

INTRODUCTION

The games in this book are designed to help learners use English in a manner that is interactive, autonomous, and purpose-driven.

Games

Here are some definitions from top experts in game design:

- A game is a system in which players engage in an artificial conflict, defined by rules, that results in a quantifiable outcome. (Salen & Zimmerman, 2004)

- A game is a form of art in which participants, termed *players*, make decisions in order to manage resources through game tokens in the pursuit of a goal. (Costikyan, 1994)

- To play a game is to engage in activity directed toward bringing about a specific state of affairs, using only means permitted by specific rules, where the means permitted by the rules are more limited in scope than they would be in the absence of the rules, and where the sole reason for accepting such limitation is to make possible such activity. (Suits, 1978)

- When you strip away the genre differences and the technological complexities, all games share four defining traits: a goal, rules, a feedback system, and voluntary participation. (McGonigal, 2012)

When students play the games in this book, they will use English in a manner that is authentic within the game world. They have to make choices during the game, and therefore determine which language skills to use in order to carry out their decisions.

The teacher is a guide during the games, ready to step in to assist with communication. The teacher may choose to note any difficulties students experience, and review these areas at a later time.

Serious Games

Serious games have a purpose beyond mere entertainment. Although a game should be fun, it can also educate. Ian Bogost calls this "procedural rhetoric," meaning that "[t]he art of persuasion through rule-based representations and interactions, rather than the spoken word, writing, images, or moving pictures" (Bogost, 2007).

Many serious game designers, such as those at Games for Change (games-forchange.org), Persuasive Games (persuasivegames.com), and Tiltfactor (tilt-factor.org), believe that games are a unique art form allowing us to understand new ideas by experiencing them interactively. (Students might even enjoy being assigned to play the games on these websites as homework!)

Organization of the Book

There are two main sections in this book.

1. Introductory games

The introductory games encourage students to find deeper connections with each other. Students need to spend a lot of time practicing the language, working and speaking in pairs or small groups. These activities can be more enjoyable when the students feel that they know each other personally. This is particularly important if they see each other only during their English classes, for example, in a language institute or a university, where they may not have other classes together.

The introductory games are designed to build cohesiveness in a class. These games involve exploring likes and dislikes, past experiences and dreams for the future, and ethics and values.

The teacher should encourage each student to participate. However, some students need to be reassured that they do not have to share anything they might feel uncomfortable discussing. As always, the teacher must exercise caution and show sensitivity to students' backgrounds and experiences. Above all, the teacher should strive to make the classroom a place of joy and peace.

2. Games to promote critical and creative thinking about the world

The games in this section focus on world issues of great importance and current relevance.

Although some games focus on cultures and contexts that may be distant from the students' everyday reality, this does not diminish their importance as topics for reflection and discussion.

Each game promotes what the Partnership for 21st Century Learning refers to as the 4 Cs: Creativity, Communication, Collaboration, and Critical thinking. The students must work together, analyzing the situations in the game in order to create solutions. They must then test these solutions in order to evaluate their choices critically.

Organization of each game

Each game section is divided into the following parts:

Purpose of the game

This section provides a short explanation of the educational value of the game

Game objective

This section gives a brief explanation of the learning objective for the game, apart from the objective of learning the English language itself.

End point of the game

Some games conclude when one team or player has won. Others require every player to achieve a particular goal.

Type of game

There is a wide variety of game-types in this book, including card games, board games, physical games, and discussion games.

Number of players

Most games allow for an unlimited number of players, however, some require players to play individually, in pairs, or in small groups.

Level/age of players

Most of the games in this book have been designed explicitly for teenagers and adults due to the subject matter. Players should ideally have at least an intermediate level of English in order to facilitate communication.

Preparation time

Some of the game resources, such as cards and boards, are provided here for the teacher to print. However, in most cases, only an example is provided so that students may design their own boards and cards and other necessary materials. Materials preparation is a vital experience in which the students consider the issues presented by the game and prepare themselves linguistically for the challenges ahead.

Playing time

Most games will take approximately one class period to play; each game includes introductory and follow up activities.

Materials and space

Most of the games require no more than the basic furniture and materials found in a classroom, though some might require space for physical movement as well.

Instructions

Each game comes with complete instructions, including how to introduce the game (the "before the game" section), how to play the game (marked under "the game") and a section with "follow-up tasks" in speaking and writing.

Important Note: The games in this book are meant to entertain and educate. However, some of the games in this book deal with issues that may be sensitive for certain students. Each teacher knows their students best and so can decide which games to skip or modify so that all the students feel comfortable and enjoy the lesson.

* * *

About pronouns in this book: We use the pronoun "they" as a singular pronoun, referring to people of any gender. This avoids the awkward and inaccurate "he or she, him or her" dichotomy.

GAME 1

A G E

Why play the game

We often make assumptions about other people based on our own experiences. For example, many people who enjoyed school find it difficult to understand people who have unpleasant memories of their school days. This game encourages players to compare their life experiences in and out of school at specific ages. Note: some students may have experienced difficult or traumatic events in their childhood. They should still be encouraged to participate in the game, but the teacher should explain that each player only reveals what they feel comfortable discussing.

Game objective

To compare life experiences

End point of the game

There is no "win" state in this game; the discussion ends when the cards have been exhausted or the time given has elapsed.

Type of game

Card

Number of players

Any size group divided into pairs (and one group of three if necessary)

Level/age of players

Beginner and up, all ages

Preparation time

5 minutes

Playing time

30-60 minutes

Materials and space

Arrange the tables and chairs so that students can comfortably sit in pairs, perhaps with soft background music playing. Each player will need a pen or pencil and one sheet of paper.

Instructions

Before the game:

1. Before the class meets, ask students to find pictures of themselves when they were younger. Ask each to bring in one photo of themselves as a baby and one as a young child. (Printed photos work best.) The students post their pictures on the walls or leave them on a center table. Everyone tries to guess whose photos they are.

2. Introduce the topic of the game by reading out sentences and asking students to raise their hands if they agree. For example, you could say:

   - Most young children enjoy spending time with their families.
   - Most children between the age of 5 and 10 enjoy school.
   - Most teenagers enjoy school.
   - Most teenagers are rebellious.

(The teacher may add to and modify these sentences if desired.)

Students then make their own sentences beginning with "Most children…" or "Most teenagers…". Each student reads their sentences aloud to the class and the rest vote on whether they agree or disagree with them.

THE GAME

Each player cuts one sheet of paper into 12 cards and marks them as follows (downloadable/photocopiable version found at http://wayzgoosepress.com/wp-content/uploads/2016/09/Social-Change-Game-1.pdf).

5	6	7	8
9	10	11	12
13	14	15	16

Note: Each number represents an age; therefore, if the students are younger than 16, the cards will only be numbered up to their current age. In a class of older adults, the cards should be numbered only to 16, so that the focus remains on the players' younger years.

1. Players sit in pairs, ideally not too close to other pairs, so that they can hear each other easily. Playing soft background music such as Mozart helps minimize distractions.

2. Each player shuffles their own deck of cards. Then, each player places their deck on the table in front of them. On the count of three, both players draw their top cards at the same time. If the cards show different numbers, players continue to draw until both cards show the same number. If the cards show the same number, the players compare their life experiences at the age shown on the cards. They may talk for as long as they wish.

3. When the pair of players has exhausted their discussion, they discard the cards with the number they have discussed. Then they draw again and repeat the process outlined in step 3. If they finish drawing all of the cards in the deck before they have discussed all of the numbers on the cards, they may shuffle their respective decks and continue to draw cards.

4. The game continues until all of the numbers on the cards have been discussed, or until the teacher calls a stop to the game.

Follow-up tasks

Speaking: Each pair creates a Venn diagram showing the similarities and differences they noted during the game between themselves and their partners. The class can then use these diagrams for a full-group discussion on what they all have in common. For example:

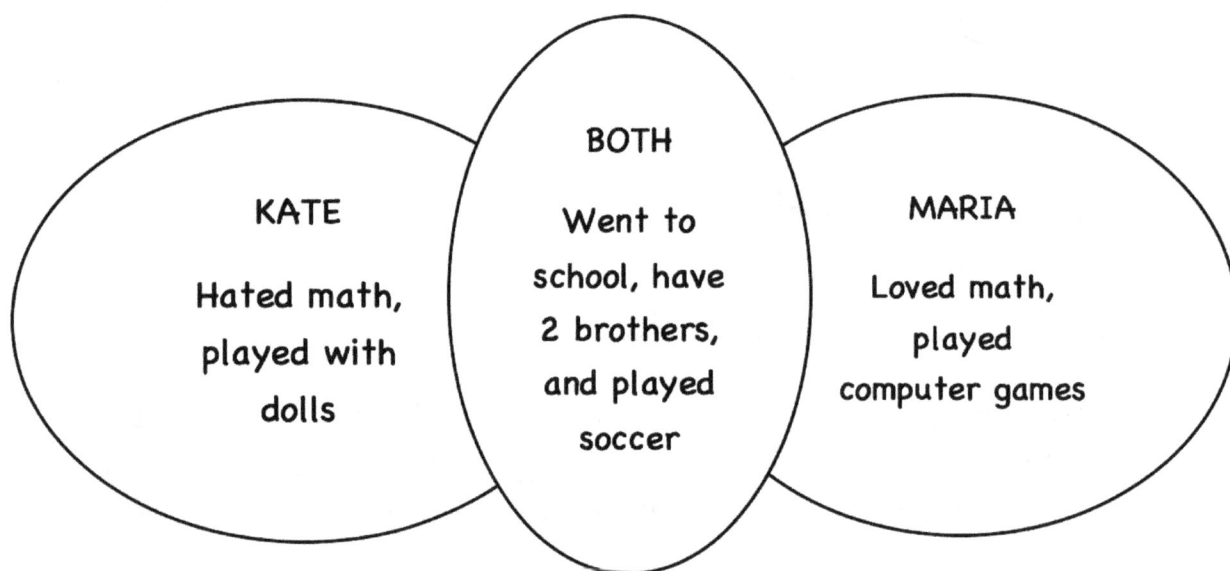

KATE

Hated math, played with dolls

BOTH

Went to school, have 2 brothers, and played soccer

MARIA

Loved math, played computer games

Writing: Students write a short essay on the similarities and differences between their childhood and those of their classmates. They may also choose to represent their ideas in the form of a group collage composed of photos of themselves and their classmates at the different ages discussed in the game. Each group of photos should have captions explaining the similarities and differences.

GAME 2

FAVORITE WORD

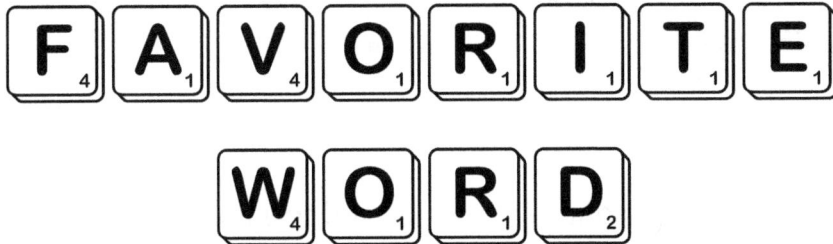

Why play the game

This game helps to review vocabulary as well as to build interpersonal relationships with classmates.

Game objective

To guess the word your partner is thinking of

End point of the game

The players both guess the words the other is thinking of.

Type of game

Guessing

Number of players

Unlimited but players play in pairs

Level/age of players

Beginner and up, all ages

Preparation time

None

Playing time

10 minutes

Materials and space required

Something to write on in front of the class, such as a whiteboard, chalkboard, or flip charts, as well as chalk or markers. All students should be comfortably seated so they can see.

Instructions

Before the game: This game works best if the teacher has previously given a vocabulary lesson. Students should study the words and understand their use and meaning.

T H E   G A M E

Students call out words they know until there is a random assortment of about 20 words on the board.

1. Ask students to choose one of the words (silently) that they like best.

2. In pairs, students try to guess what word their partner chose, and why.

3. Take a vote on which words were the most popular in this task.

Follow-up tasks

Speaking: Students make up a song or a rap using as many of the words, and their reasons for liking them, as possible.

Writing: Students write a fairy tale or a children's story using the vocabulary. Then they illustrate the story and include a mini-dictionary with the meanings of the words.

GAME 3

N U M B E R S

Why play the game

It is interesting to see how people represent themselves, their priorities, and their values. In ice-breaker activities, people are asked to capture their own essence and to decide how much to show of themselves, often in very few words. This forces them to think about what aspects of themselves to present. This is a short guessing game for students to get to know each other using symbols to represent what they feel is important to them.

Game objective

To guess what the numbers chosen by your partner represent

End point of the game

When each person has guessed the meaning of all of their partner's numbers.

Type of game

Guessing

Number of players

Unlimited but players play in pairs, finding new partners when they finish.

Level/age of players

Beginner and up, all ages

Preparation time

None

Playing time

10 minutes

Materials and space required

A classroom where students can mingle

Instructions

Before the game: Demonstrate the game to students by writing four numbers on the board that are important to you (for example, age, children, number of languages you speak, number of years teaching experience, etc.). For example:

40   3   4   14

T H E   G A M E

1. Players write down four numbers that are important to them. Encourage the not to take too much time for this part.

2. In pairs, each player tries to guess what each number represents to their partner. They can give each other hints if necessary.

3. Players who finish can search for a new partner and repeat the game.

4. Before ending the game, the teacher should give everyone 30 seconds to tell their partner the answers.

Follow-up tasks

Speaking: This game can be played with names of family members. For example, a player might write:

José Zoe Mick Wally

The player's partner must guess that these are the names of the player's husband, daughter, grandfather, and dog, respectively.

They can also write names of songs that relate to a special event in their lives, names of places where special events took place, or names of brands or products they feel are important to them.

Writing: Students compose a poem about their partner, using the information they've learned, but without mentioning the partner's name. For example:

> Four years since her baby was born
> Four dogs sleep on her lawn
> Fourteen years since she met the love of her life
> Fourteen years since she became his wife.
> José is the lucky man's name
> And that's what I learned about X from playing this game!

GAME 4

POINT OF VIEW GRAMMAR

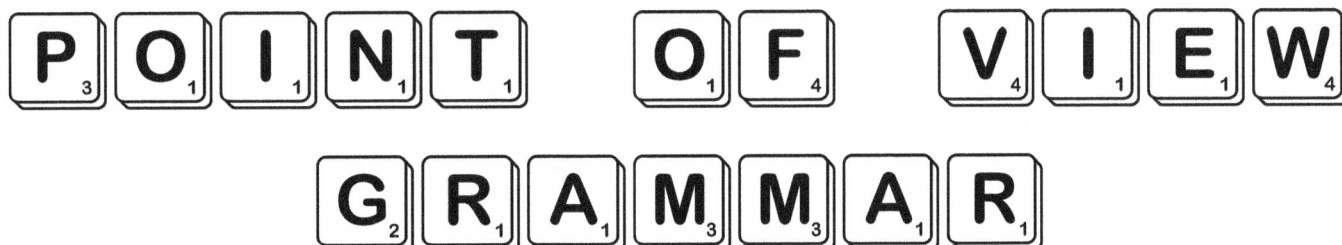

Why play the game

Emotional intelligence, among other things, means being able to empathize with others and to see the world from their perspective. Most English exercise books ask students to write sentences about themselves, but this game asks them to write sentences about others, perhaps without knowing much about them.

Game objective

To guess how your partner will complete the sentences without speaking or looking at each other.

End point of the game

The winner is the player who has correctly guessed the highest number of their partner's sentences.

Type of game

Guessing

Number of players

Unlimited but players play in pairs

Level/age of players

Beginner and up, all ages

Preparation time

None

Playing time

10 minutes

Materials and space required

Classroom with desks and chairs for everyone, pen and paper for each player

Instructions

Before the game: The teacher selects grammar points and writes them as sentence starters. For example,

- Every morning, I…
- Last weekend, I…
- In five years, I…
- I have never…
- I would never…
- If I had one million dollars, I would…
- I shouldn't have…

T H E   G A M E

Players form pairs with someone they don't know very well. They should sit across the room from their partner and try to imagine how their partner will have completed the sentences:

- Every morning, he/she…

- Last weekend, he/she…

- In five years, he/she…

- He/she has never…

- He/she would never…

- If he/she had one million dollars, he/she would…

- He/she shouldn't have…

Players compare answers with their partner.

Follow-up tasks

Speaking: The teacher redistributes the sentences from the game among the class. Students take turns reading sentences aloud while the class tries to guess who the sentences refer to.

Writing: Students work individually or in pairs to try to complete the sentences from the teacher's point of view. The teacher, in addition to correcting the grammar, notes which answers are true and which are not.

GAME 5

P E R S O N A L

P O S T E R

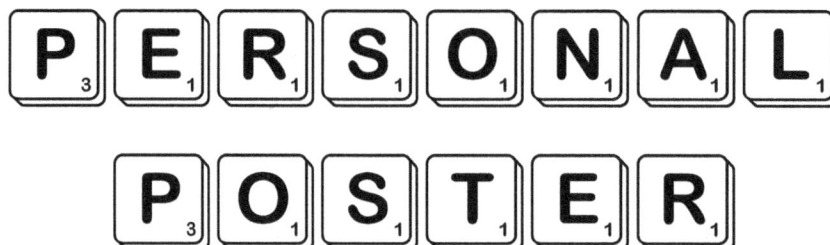

Why play the game

One of the challenges of an English class is for everyone to get to know one another, and for the teacher to get to know the students as human beings, not just as students. A student-designed quiz allows students to practice question forms (arguably the toughest grammar point of them all!) in a highly creative and personalized manner. Some students will make their questions relatively easy for others to answer, others will deliberately write fiendishly difficult ones, regardless of their language level and ability. This game gives students a nice chance to find old photos and create a narrative of their life to share with the class.

Game objective

To answer questions about classmates

End point of the game

The winner is the team who has answered the most questions correctly

Type of game

Question and answer

Number of players

5 to 30

Level/age of players

Beginner and up, all ages

Preparation time

1 or 2 days at home to prepare the posters

Playing time

20 minutes

Materials and space required

Classroom with space to place the posters on the tables or walls. Players need pen and paper.

Instructions

Before the game: Each player makes a poster with photographs of themselves and captions explaining why they feel these photographs are important to them. Then, on a separate paper, they write five questions, the answers to which can be found on their poster.

On the day of the game, students put their posters on the wall and hand the questions to the teacher.

The players are given time to study each other's posters without knowing what the questions are. They can ask each other about the photos.

THE GAME

Players divide into two teams. Each team sends a player to the front of the class as a team representative. The teacher reads a question aloud. Whichever team representative hits the table first may have a chance to try to answer. If the answer is correct, the team has a point. If the answer is incorrect, the other team representative may try.

Then each team selects a new team representative and the game continues until the teacher has asked all of the questions.

Follow-up tasks

Speaking: Students mingle freely after this task to find out more about each other and ask further questions about the posters.

Writing: Students award prizes to each other using the following template:

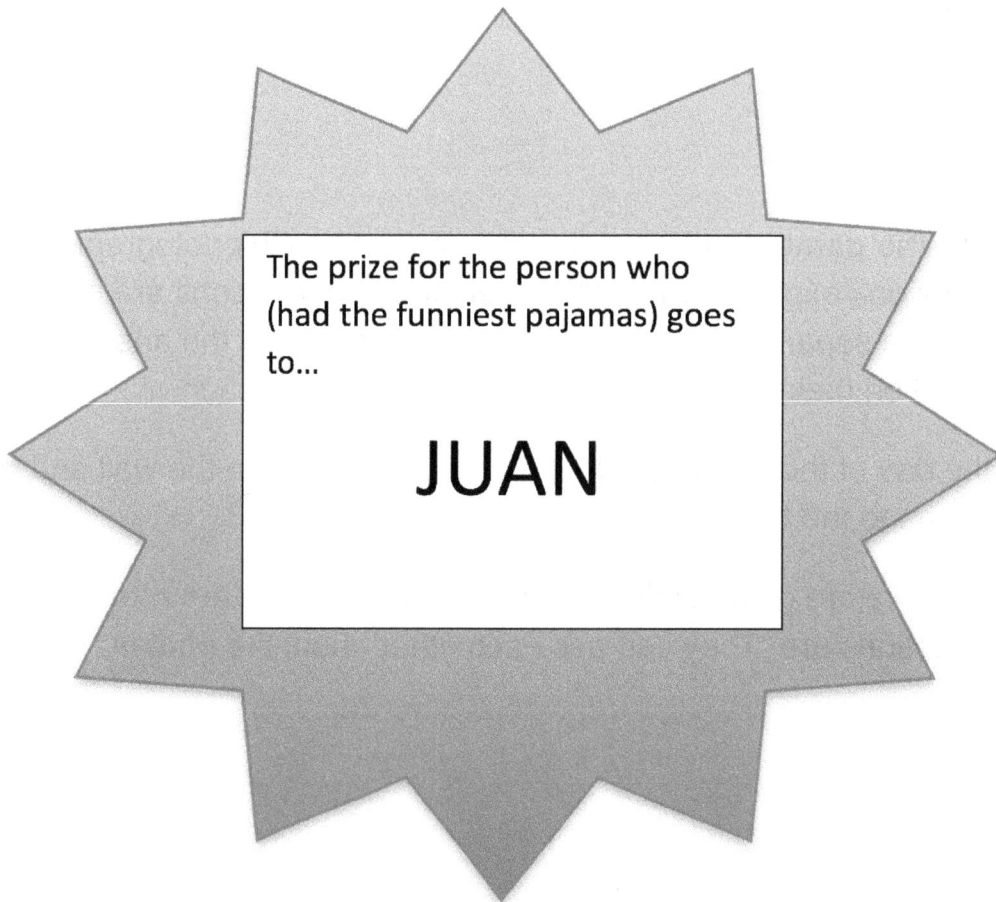

The prize for the person who (had the funniest pajamas) goes to...

JUAN

GAME 6

S T A N D   S I T

Why play the game

Blind obedience has resulted in horrific atrocities; think, for example, of the Nazis and other acts of genocide. The Nuremberg defense, that is, "I was only following orders," is not an acceptable excuse.

In class, students have to follow their teacher's orders, but students need to trust that the teacher's assignment will benefit them before they will do it. This is why it may be beneficial for students to get to know their instructors, from their CVs and their experience, to their teaching philosophies and their values, and so on.

This is a short, physical game, testing how well students follow orders (no matter how silly).

Game objective

To follow orders

End point of the game

When everyone has successfully followed the sequence of orders

Type of game

Physical

Number of players

Unlimited

Level/age of players

Beginner and up, all ages

Preparation time

None

Playing time

5 minutes

Materials and space required

A classroom with space to stand and sit

Instructions

Before the game: It is a good idea to play this game as early as possible at the start of the course you are teaching. It is best when the teacher starts the game suddenly, and with no warning whatsoever.

THE GAME

Tell the players the following:

Please stand up.

Thank you. Now please sit down.

Stand up, sit down.

Stand up, sit down, pull your hair.

Stand up, sit down, pull your hair, touch your shoe.

Stand up, sit down, pull your hair, touch your shoe, hit the table.

Stand up, sit down, pull your hair, touch your shoe, hit the table, raise your hands.

Stand up, sit down, pull your hair, touch your shoe, hit the table, raise your hands, say hello.

Follow-up tasks

Speaking: The teacher organizes a debate by dividing the class in two teams. One team must argue that students should always obey a teacher. The other team will argue that there are times when it may be appropriate *not* to do what a teacher says.

Writing: Students write in their journals about a time when they obeyed an authority figure and later regretted it, and a time when they disobeyed an authority figure and regretted it. Optionally, they read each other's journals and discuss them.

GAME 7

VALUES

Why play the game

Everyone has certain beliefs and values they hold dear. However, it is difficult to know the values in words and clearly see their boundaries. For example, most people claim to believe in honesty, but wouldn't dream of telling "the whole truth and nothing but the truth," because sometimes the truth hurts people's feelings unnecessarily.

This is a game about defining our values and making metaphorical connections between images and ideas. It's also about seeing how someone else may perceive the same concept differently than we do.

Game objective

To identify another player's values and anti-values

End point of the game

The first person to place their partner's value stickers correctly on their collage wins, or the one who gets the most right wins.

Type of game

Picture identification

Number of players

Unlimited but players play in pairs

Level/age of players

Intermediate and up, teenagers and older

Preparation time

1 or 2 days to make the collage

Playing time

10 minutes

Materials and space required

A classroom with space to place the posters on the tables or walls. Players need pen and paper, and 10 plain white labels.

Instructions

Before the game: Each player thinks of five of their values and five of their anti-values; they write one word per label so that they have ten labels, one word on each. Students should not peel the labels off the backing.

Then, they go to Google Images or other photo services and find pictures that represent those values and anti-values. They will use their photos to make a collage. They should try not to make the images obvious. For example, for *dishonesty*, an image of a student sneakily looking at his classmate's test paper would be obvious. However, an image of a person with the face blurred might be a little more challenging.

T H E   G A M E

Players play in pairs. First, they exchange collages. The first person to place their partner's value stickers under the correct images on the collage wins, or the one who gets the most right wins.

Follow-up tasks

Speaking: The students ask each other about the relevance of the images they chose. They then compare their similarities and differences.

Writing: Students choose one of their words and write a poem. Each line of the poem should begin with a letter of the word they have chosen. For example, if the student has chosen *racism* as an anti-value, they might write:

R is for how ridiculous it is to believe in the superiority of one race

*A*ll of us are equal

*C*rosses burned to frighten people only show the ignorance of the burners

I believe in justice for everyone

*S*o spread the word

*M*y skin color is beautiful, and so is yours

GAME 8

A₁ D₂ D₂ I₁ C₃ T₁ E₁ D₂

Why play the game

> This game promotes tolerance for people addicted to drugs, alcohol, cigarettes, food, surgery, etc., while at the same time, warning of the dangers of addiction by having the players imagine themselves as addicts.

Game objective

> To imagine themselves leading secret lives as addicts by journaling their imaginary experience--from the first time they try the addictive substance or behavior until the moment they are finally convinced to quit.

End point of the game

> When the players role play "confessing" their addictions to the other players, who act as concerned friends and family.

Type of game

> Alternate reality and role play; meaning that everything is the same in players' lives except for one crucial detail; in this case, the players imagine that they live their real lives while hiding a secret addiction.

Number of players

> Unlimited. Players play individually with the teacher. The final role play is done in small groups.

Level/age of players

Students should be at an intermediate level of English. The game works best if players are older than 16.

Preparation time

5 to 10 minutes for the teacher to explain the game

Playing time

1 to 5 class periods

Materials and space required

Players need pen and paper. The classroom may be organized into a small-group configuration for the final role-play.

Instructions

Before the game: The teacher may wish to introduce the game by showing a video of someone describing an addiction they have. Alternately, the teacher may wish to begin by giving a speech similar to the following (in a manner to show that the teacher is not being serious):

> I have a confession to make, and I would prefer you not tell the school authorities what I am about to share with you. I am secretly addicted to cocaine and nobody, not even my family knows. Usually I can hide it with no-one the wiser, but sometimes when I've used cocaine before class I find myself talking very fast (here the teacher speeds up the speech) and my thoughts begin to race and I have trouble controlling them. Other times when I haven't been able to get my dose of cocaine I find myself getting very irritable (here the teacher pretends to make an angry face) and I get very angry when I see that students are not paying attention. I know that I need help, but I'm honestly not sure that I'm ready to quit yet.

THE GAME

Players individually write in a journal describing how their "addiction" began. They then describe their previous weekend as it happened in reality, but imagining how they felt about either being able to indulge in their addiction, or alternatively, being *un*able to indulge in it. They may require time to research the effects of the drug before writing. They may write various journal entries in this style over the next few lessons, perhaps explaining how they dealt with work or school or their family lives while attempting to keep their addiction a secret. The teacher should respond to each journal entry by asking questions to help the players further develop their character.

Follow-up tasks

Speaking: Players research how Alcoholics Anonymous meetings are conducted. They then form groups of 4-5 players who will all act as friends. Each player stands up to make their "confession" in character and receive encouragement and sympathy from the other players in their group.

Writing: Students write a final essay or journal entry as their real selves, explaining what they learned from playing the game.

They may also continue with a final presentation, in which they inform the rest of the class of the causes and effects of the addiction they chose in the game. This will be particularly effective if they find and include pictures of the most extreme effects of the addiction, or if they include stories of celebrities who have experienced this addiction.

GAME 9

B₃ **A**₁ **S**₁ **K**₅ **E**₁ **T**₁   **C**₃ **A**₁ **S**₁ **E**₁

Why play the game

This is a game about the root causes of inequality.

We live in a culture which we are taught is a meritocracy--if you work hard, you will be successful and get ahead. However, reality is never that simple. The privileged among us never realize how much the less fortunate must overcome in order to succeed.

As an example, consider the case of someone whose family is successful and has a lot of money, and can afford to send them to a "good" school. This person will make friends at this school who come from the same sorts of families. When these children grow up, they will have powerful connections enabling them to have easier access to the sorts of jobs and lives that are considered successful. If these people work hard, they will surely succeed.

In this game, these people are represented by those who are physically closest to the basket. The players in the back represent the people who must overcome such barriers as racism, sexism, poverty and other difficulties.

Most games are played on a premise of equality. For example, teams of ten year-old girls do not usually play football against teams of 18 year-old men. This game is particularly shocking because it begins with players in *unequal* positions.

In this game, those at the front will see the goal. Those at the back will see the obstacles.

Game objective

To understand the basis of inequality

End point of the game

The winners are those who manage to throw their paper in the basket

Type of game

Physical/Basketball

Number of players

10 to 30

Level/age of players

Beginner and up, 10 and older

Preparation time

None

Playing time

5 minutes

Materials and space required

A basket or empty garbage can at the front of the room, a ball (can be made out of paper), desks and chairs arranged in rows.

Instructions

Before the game: This game works best if the teacher gives no advance warning or preparation.

THE GAME

Without moving from their seats, students try to throw the ball into the wastepaper basket at the front of the room.

Follow-up tasks

Speaking: Students list and discuss all of the reasons why the game was unfair. For example, in addition to being farther from the basket, some students may argue that girls are disadvantaged because some girls do not throw as well as boys, or they are not as tall. The teacher should encourage the students to come up with other reasons.

Writing: Students write in a journal about how this game highlights inequality and discrimination.

GAME 10

B₃ I₁ G₂ B₃ U₁ S₁ I₁ N₁ E₁ S₁ S₁

Why play the game

One way that mega-companies operate is to crowd out small, independently owned businesses. One major coffee chain, for example, uses the term *cannibalizing* to describe its policy of putting so many of its coffee shops in a relatively small area that it effectively pushes all of its competitors out of business. The result, as Naomi Klein points out in her book *No Logo,* is that small businesses are driven to bankruptcy, which destroys local communities and leaves consumers with no real choice as to where to shop.

Game objective

The aim of the game is to encourage students to question how much expansion and competitiveness really help or hurt the market.

End point of the game

When all of the players are part of the chain

Type of game

Playground "chain tag"

Number of players

10 to 20

Level/age of players

Teenagers and older, intermediate and higher

Preparation time

None

Playing time

5 to 10 minutes

Materials and space required

An outdoor play area

Instructions

Before the game: This game works best if the teacher gives no advance warning or preparation.

THE GAME

This game is based on the playground game of chain tag. One person is "it" and attempts to catch other players. When the person who is "it" touches another player, they join hands and together become "it" and run off in search of other players. The game continues until everyone is part of the giant "it" chain.

Follow-up tasks

Speaking: Students can discuss the answer to the question: "What does this game have to do with big business?"

Writing: Students research the cases of Starbucks, Walmart, McDonald's, or other well-known companies in their country. They write a case study in which they describe what happened in a specific case when a large chain arrived in a neighborhood. For example, they can describe what happens to local farmers' markets and "mom-and-pop" grocery stores when a large supermarket arrives in a particular area. Do the smaller shops close? Do more people come to live in the neighborhood? What happens to the local food culture? Etc.

GAME 11

C₃ A₁ R₁ P₃ E₁   D₂ I₁ E₁ M₃

Why play the game

Carpe diem is Latin for "seize the day," a command to live each moment and make it count.

Game objective

To remember how precious and short life is

End point of the game

To write as much as possible before time runs out

Type of game

Writing

Number of players

5 to 30

Level/age of players

Teenagers and older, intermediate and higher

Preparation time

None

Playing time

One minute

Materials and space required

A classroom with desks and chairs for all players, pens and paper

Instructions

Before the game: This game works best if the teacher gives no advance warning or preparation.

THE GAME

Students take out pen and paper. Instruct them to write a letter to someone they love, telling them how they feel. After one minute, stop them.

Follow-up tasks

Speaking: Students discuss the answers to the following questions: "Did you write everything you wanted to? What else did you want to say in your letter? Have you said these things to the person already? If not, why not?"

The class watches a clip from the movie *Dead Poets Society* (youtube.com/watch?v=veYR3ZC9wMQ), and answers the question: "What does *carpe diem* mean?"

They can also listen to the song "Time" (youtube.com/watch?v=A7pI96Osp9c) by Pink Floyd (note, the words begin at minute 2:42) and discuss the relevance of the song to the idea of *carpe diem*.

Writing: Students research the meaning of *carpe diem*. They work individually or in pairs to select the best lines from songs and poetry on the topic *of carpe diem*. They copy these lines in an artistic way onto a poster to hang on a wall of the classroom.

GAME 12

CULTURE JAMMERS

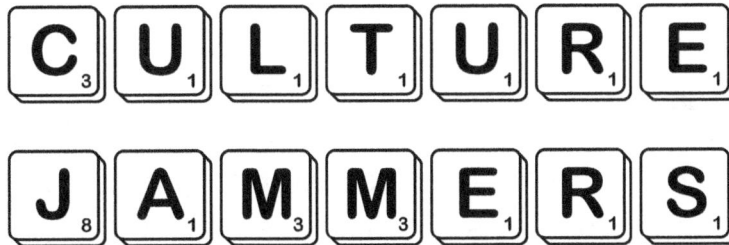

Why play the game

Culture jamming is a way to use a company's or organization's own advertising to show its harmful practices. The aim is to get people to think about the values these companies hold and to compare them to the values they claim to have.

The aim of this game is to have students explore the values that companies advertise, along with their counter-narrative. For example, the values that many fast food restaurants sell in their marketing is essentially "happy time for families and kids." However, some might think that they have unsustainable production ethics, poor treatment of workers, or unhealthy menu choices that belie these values.

Culture-jammers often use words in their slogans that are very similar to the original slogan, usually changing only one or two words to make their point. For example, they change the words of McDonald's slogan "I'm lovin' it" to "I'm gainin' it" to focus on how people might get fat if they eat too much junk food. Culture-jammers often do the same with images: they change only one or two things about the original image to make their point, such as making Ronald Mc-Donald, the clown in the McDonald's advertisements, fat instead of thin.

Richard Garfield, the man who designed the card game "Magic: The Gathering," wrote of the idea of the meta-game (Garfield, 2000). This idea means that players think about the game not only during the play, but also before the game, between games and after the game. In this game, the players themselves make the cards, and this gives them time to think about the concept of culture jamming, and how it highlights anti-values in business.

Game objective

The aim is to collect a set of cards with the product, the logo, the slogan, and the culture jammed slogan.

End point of the game

The winner is the first player to collect, through game play, a set of cards with the product, the logo, the slogan and the culture jammed slogan.

Type of game

Card game, similar to gin rummy

Number of players

Unlimited, but players play in groups of 3-5

Level/age of players

Beginner and up, teenagers and older

Preparation time

1 to 2 hours

Playing time

20 minutes

Materials and space required

Players should sit comfortably around a table in groups of 4 or 5 so that each player can reach the cards in the center.

Instructions

Before the game: The game works best if students take the time to design their own cards, while researching the companies they are interested in. Here are some examples for the cards with the product, the logo, the slogan, and the culture-jammed slogan:

- Hamburgers and fast food / McDonald's logo / "I'm lovin' it" / "I'm gainin' it"
- Sports shoes / Nike "swoosh" / "Just do it" /"Just do it" (with an image of a child worker)
- Computers, iPads, iPhones / Apple logo / "Think different" / image of people chained by their ankles by the trademark white headphones
- Soda / Coca Cola logo / "Enjoy Coca Cola" / "Enjoy Capitalism"
- The students are in groups of 4-5. Each player makes cards with the product, the logo, the slogan and the culture jammed slogan for four different companies. The players must communicate so that the cards are not repeated.

All of the finished cards are then shuffled together.

T H E   G A M E

Each player is dealt four cards. The rest of the deck is placed face down. The first player picks one card from the deck and discards one of the cards in their hand. The next player may either pick up the first player's discarded card or take one from the face down deck. The players continue taking turns picking up and discarding cards around the table until one player gets a set of cards with the product, the logo, the slogan, and the culture-jammed slogan.

Follow-up tasks

Speaking: After the game, students discuss what they have learned about the companies, and what they feel about what they have learned.

Writing: Students work in pairs to create their own culture jams using images and slogans. They can post them on social media, or around the class or building. The culture jams work best if they also include a short paragraph to explain what the image is about.

GAME 13

DUMB WAYS TO DIE

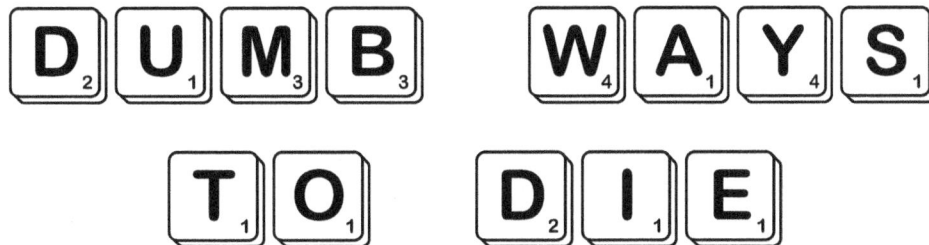

Why play the game

There is a popular free phone game, as well as a music video called "Dumb Ways to Die" (dumbwaystodie.com). The point of the game is to teach people to avoid accidents. There is some debate (*The Best of Global Digital Marketing*, 2016) as to whether this campaign was effective at reducing train accidents; however, there seems to be little doubt that the game is fun and worked well as an example of a viral advertising campaign.

This game has a similar aim. Players read and think about stories from "The Darwin Awards" (darwinawards.com) website, in which people die in very stupid ways. The stories are funny, but also serve as a warning to others not to make the same mistakes.

Game objective

To think about dangerous actions

End point of the game

The winner is the last player left telling stories without repeating someone else's story.

Type of game

Storytelling

Number of players

Unlimited, but players play in groups of 4-5

Level/age of players

Intermediate and up, teenagers and older

Preparation time

None

Playing time

60 minutes

Materials and space required

Classroom space. Each player needs pen and paper.

Instructions

Before the game: Students can play the "Dumb ways to Die" game and watch the video (dumbwaystodie.com), then follow up with this game.

Players read as many stories as they can from "The Darwin Awards" website (darwinawards.com) in a given amount of time (approximately two hours). They summarize each story that they read, using a single sentence with the past unreal conditional. For example, "If Kevin Sprint hadn't tried to cross the speed racing track, he wouldn't have been hit by the car."

T₁H₄E₁ G₂A₁M₃E₁

Players play in groups of 4-5. Each player in the group takes turns telling their stories. They may not look at the stories or at any notes about the stories except for their one-sentence summaries in the second conditional. They must not repeat a story that anyone in the group has already told previously. The other members of the group listen and try to reconstruct the original past unreal conditional sentence based on the story.

The winner in each group is the player who tells the most stories. The winners from each group can then go a final round with the winners of the other circles.

Follow-up tasks

Speaking: Students vote on which of all of the stories they heard was the funniest.

Writing: Students write an essay entitled "dumb ways teenagers die." Each essay should concern a dangerous activity that teenagers and young people participate in, such as smoking or texting while driving a car. When the essays are ready, they exchange them with a classmate who then adds humorous illustrations. The class can donate the essays to a local high school, or post them in their classroom or school.

GAME 14

FIRST PERSON SHOOTER

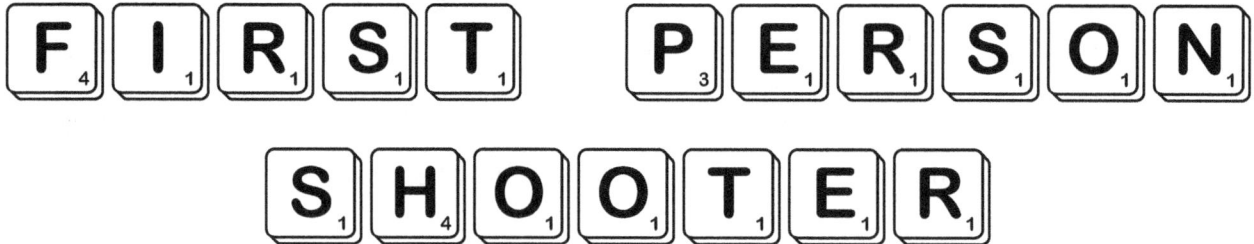

Why play the game

Many people enjoy movies or video games about war. There are claims that watching and participating in such fictitious violence can desensitize and numb people to real violence, although these claims have not been proven. On the contrary, in many war games the player is faced with ethical dilemmas that mirror the real worlds of war and diplomacy. In a war game, the player is often required to adopt different sorts of identities, from the foot soldier in the thick of war, to the general plotting strategy. In many games, it is often unclear who the "good guys" are and who the "villains" are, and the player must change their perspective in light of events and plot developments (Gee, 2003).

This is an interactive storytelling game in which the aim is to help the character survive, while behaving as ethically as possible. However, given that a "choose your own adventure story" (Packard, 1979-1998) is a story in which the reader makes their own choices, it can be equally interesting to explore the negative side, choosing a story that highlights anti-values.

Game objective

To make choices as they are presented in the story

End point of the game

To find the best possible ending for the story, though some players may choose to find the worst possible ending

Type of game

Interactive storytelling game

Number of players

Unlimited; players may write their stories alone or in pairs

Level/age of players

Teenagers and older, intermediate and up

Preparation time

Several classes to write and edit the stories

Playing time

Approximately 5-15 minutes per student (or pair)

Materials and space required

A classroom with a space at the front for the reader(s). Each player needs pen and paper.

Instructions

Before the game: Players work alone or in pairs to write a war story with multiple paths to multiple endings. The story should be written in the second person (you) to make it feel more "real". In order to plan the story, it helps if the players outline their story as a tree. For example,

```
                                            ┌─────────────────────┐
                                            │ You follow the child │
                                            │ back to a terrorist  │
                                            │ training camp. The   │
                                            │ child is proud of    │
                                            │ being a terrorist.   │
                            ┌──────────────┐└─────────────────────┘
                            │ The person   │
                            │ who set      │ ┌─────────────────────┐
                            │ the bomb is  │ │ You follow the child │
                            │ a 12         │ │ back to a terrorist  │
                            │ year-old     │ │ training camp the    │
                            │ Iraqi child. │ │ child wants to       │
┌──────────────┐           └──────────────┘ │ escape from.         │
│ You are in   │                            └─────────────────────┘
│ a war        │
│ zone. A bomb │           ┌──────────────┐ ┌─────────────────────┐
│ explodes     │           │ The person   │ │ The commanding       │
│ nearby.      │           │ who set      │ │ officer planted the  │
│ You try to   │           │ the bomb was │ │ bomb to kill the     │
│ find out     │           │ your own     │ │ terrorist who had    │
│ who set the  │           │ commanding   │ │ killed his own child.│
│ bomb.        │           │ officer.     │ └─────────────────────┘
└──────────────┘           └──────────────┘
```

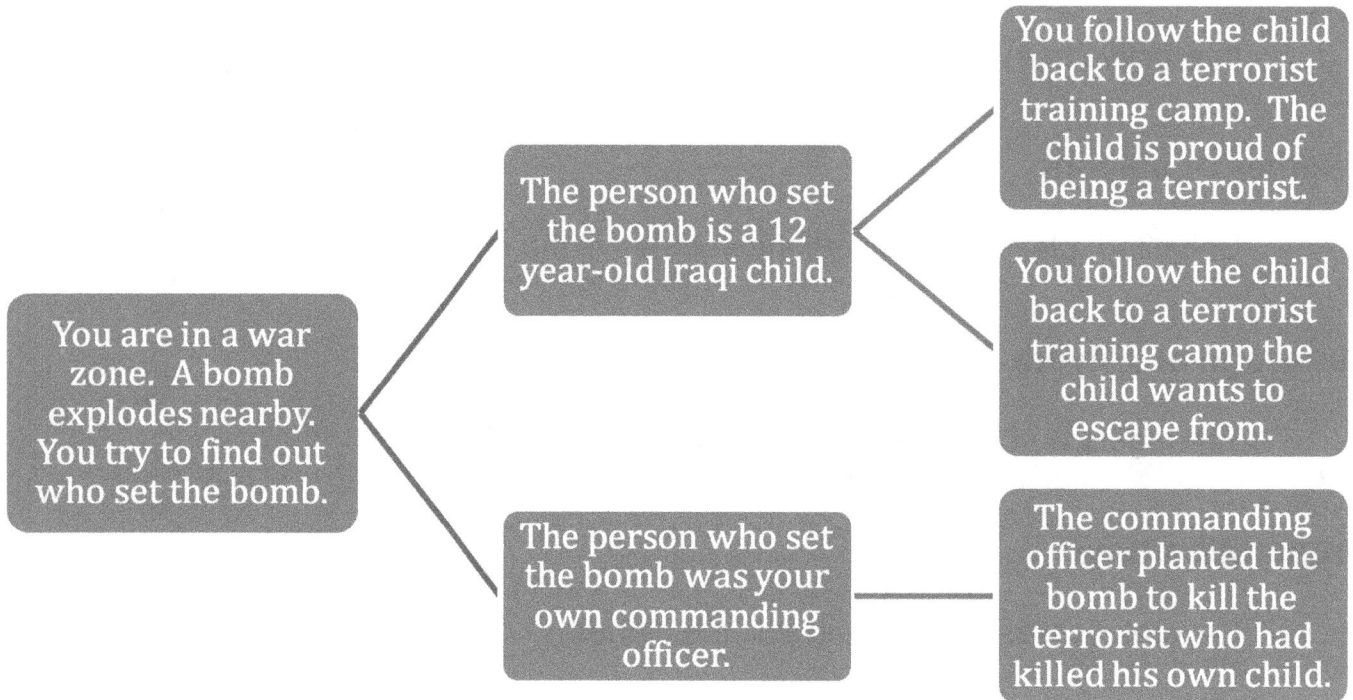

When the players write out the story, they should provide choices for their listeners. In the example above, the first segment of the story may look like this:

You are in a war zone. A bomb explodes nearby. No one is killed, but a toddler has been burned and a dog has a wounded leg. Also a car has been damaged and an apple cart has been destroyed. You try to find out who set the bomb. You see people running away. You notice a 12-year-old girl running around a corner looking behind her at the scene. There is something suspicious about the way she moves. However, you think that the bomb was thrown from behind a car across the street.

Do you want to follow the 12-year-old girl?

OR

Do you want to look behind the car across the street?

The players develop the story; the teacher can help them to edit the English. The length of the story, and of each segment within the story, should be set by the teacher, depending on the level of the learners. Of course, students can be encouraged to exceed this limit.

T H E   G A M E

Each player, or pair of players, reads their story aloud to their classmates, pausing to present the choices to their listeners who vote on which choice to make. They then continue the story accordingly.

If players have written the story in pairs, they may divide the reading as they see fit, bearing in mind that some students may not wish to read aloud before the group.

Follow-up tasks

Speaking: If the class wants, the players can reread the story from the beginning, this time allowing their classmates to make different choices until all or nearly all of the possibilities have been explored.

Writing: The students write journal entries about the stories they heard. They should note what choices they made during the story and what happened in the stories as a result of these choices. Then they can explain how they felt about the stories.

GAME 15

F O O D, I N C.

Why play the game

Food, Inc. is a powerful movie describing everything you never wanted to know about where our food comes from.

Michael Pollan, in his bestseller *The Omnivore's Dilemma* (2016), described how ubiquitous corn is, for example:

- High Fructose Corn Syrup (HFCS) is in everything from ketchup to Coca Cola.
- Cattle, who are ruminants and should only eat grass, are often fed corn
- When corn is fed to chickens, it is difficult for them to digest, which means that farmers have to feed them large amounts of antibiotics so they don't get sick. The chickens, and the people who eat them, can develop a resistance to these antibiotics, which means they can no longer protect them from disease.
- Ethanol, a corn sugar, is made into gasoline.

The list goes on. In fact, Pollan describes a McDonald's meal this way:

> This is how the laboratory measured our meal: soda (100% corn), milk shake (78%), salad dressing (65%), chicken nuggets (56%), cheeseburger (52%), and French fries (23%). (2016, p. 116)

Food, Inc. (Kenner, 2008) shows the politics of food from many different angles: the producers, the animals, and the consumers, and it contains many interviews with Michael Pollan. However, the movie itself might be a bit difficult to understand for learners. Therefore, this game aims to focus only on the problems associated with the overproduction and overuse of corn in our food system.

Game objective

In this game, the players go on a journey beginning with corn and ending at a hospital following four different routes: HFCS, beef, pork and fruits and vegetables. Each of the four players starts out as an ear of corn. Each one follows a different path: HFCS, cow feed, pig feed, transportation and refrigeration for fruits and vegetables. Along each path are cards that players can pick up to find the story.

End point of the game

The winner is the player who survives and/or has the most coins remaining.

Type of game

Board game

Number of players

2 to 4 players

Level/age of players

Teenagers and older, intermediate and up

Preparation time

Approximately 30 minutes for the teacher to prepare the board

Playing time

10 to 15 minutes

Materials and space required

The teacher should print and cut out the following cards. (downloadable/photocopiable version found at http://wayzgoosepress.com/wp-content/uploads/2016/09/Social-Change-Game-15.pdf).

PATH 1: FRUITS AND VEGETABLES	PATH 2: CHICKEN	PATH 3: HIGH FRUCTOSE CORN SYRUP	PATH 4: BEEF
Fruits and vegetables are refrigerated after picking using ethanol (corn based gas).	Chickens naturally are not vegetarian. They need insects and plants but in factory farms, they are only fed corn.	Corn is processed into HFCS (high fructose corn syrup).	Corn is fed to cows because it is cheap and it fattens them up quicker.
Fruits and vegetables are transported long distances using ethanol.	Chickens are being raised and slaughtered in less time.	The corn used has been genetically modified for use with Monsanto pesticides.	Cows are ruminants and cannot digest corn.
Fruits and vegetables are genetically modified by Monsanto which also modifies corn. For example: tomatoes are spliced with fish genes.	They are not permitted freedom and they grow so large they can't stand.	There is an attempt to rename HFCY to "corn sugar" and label it natural.	This diet produces e-coli in the cow. However, ammonia is used to kill most of it.
E-coli is found in fruits and vegetables from water contaminated by factory farms).	The farmers are often in debt to the company for $500.000 but only make $ 18000 per year.	HFCS is used in many food products including: cereals, candy bars, applesauce, canned fruits, frozen pizzas, cereal bars, tonic, and other processed foods.	Corn makes cows require antibiotics which they become resistant to.
The soil is depleted by monocultures and the fruits and vegetables no longer have as many nutrients.	Corn makes chickens need antibiotics which are eaten by the consumer.	Overconsumption of HFCS can lead to: diabetes, heart problems, obesity, or cancer.	Animals and workers are badly abused in the secrecy of the factory farm.

The teacher should copy this board:

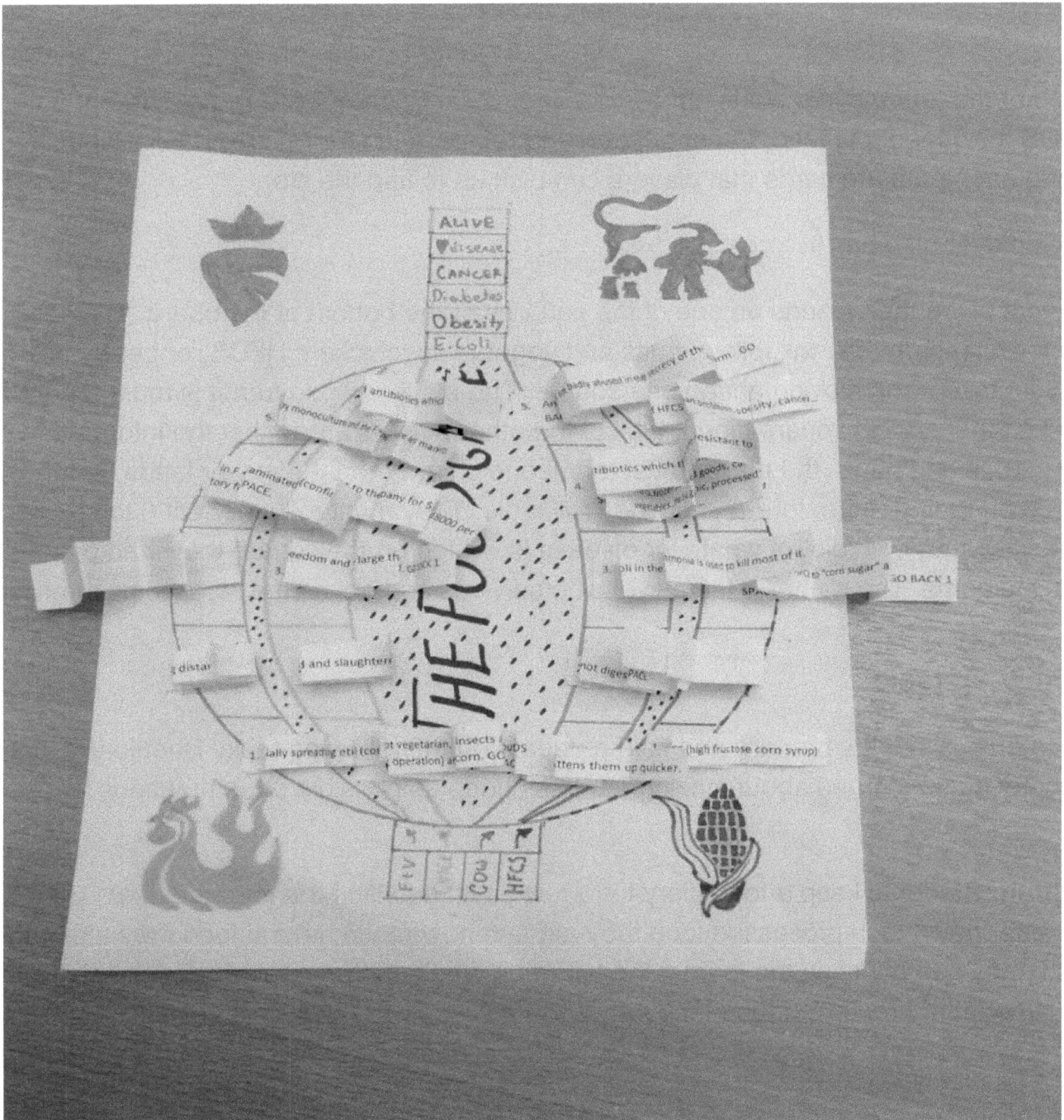

(art design by Esteban Andrés Laso Troya)

Instructions

Before the game: The students watch the *Food, Inc.* movie trailer (youtube. com/watch?v=5eKYyD14d_0) three or four times. Each time the students watch, they should note down a piece of information that surprised them.

T H E   G A M E

Each of the four players starts out as an ear of corn. Each one follows a different path: HFCS, cow feed, pig feed, transportation and refrigeration for fruits and vegetables. Along each path are cards that players can pick up to find the story.

Each player also has five coins.

Players place their tokens on one of the squares at the bottom of the board. This tells them which path they will follow: fruits and vegetables, chicken, HFCS, or beef. They players take turns moving ahead one square. The player whose turn it is must read the card on the landing square aloud. If all of the other players agree that the information on the card is bad news, the player must forfeit one coin. When the player lands on the last space on their path (before *E coli*), they roll a die. They must roll a perfect 6 to survive; otherwise they will "die" of whatever disease is written on the square they land on and lose the game. The winner is the player who survives and/or has the most coins remaining.

Follow-up tasks

Speaking: Students prepare and hold a debate on the following topic: Should the food industry be concerned about making food as cheap as possible or as nutritious as possible?

Writing: Students keep a food diary for a few days, detailing the food they eat. Then they consider how much processed food they ate and how much natural food they ate. If they wish, they can continue the journal the following week and attempt to consciously reduce the amount of processed food they eat.

GAME 16

THE GIRL EFFECT

Why play the game

A girl living in poverty is more likely to quit school, become pregnant at a young age as a child bride or as a victim of rape or prostitution, and perpetuate the cycle of poverty with her own children. See the video at youtube.com/watch?v=1e8xgF0JtVg. The premise of "the girl effect" is that it takes very little to turn around the life of a 12-year-old girl, and the consequences for not doing so can be tremendous.

Game objective

To show two alternate paths of what may happen to a disadvantaged 12-year-old

End point of the game

When the girl is either a successful adult or dead

Type of game

Board game

Number of players

2 to 4 players

Level/age of players

Intermediate and up, teenagers and older

Preparation time

Approximately 20-40 minutes to prepare the board

Playing time

10 minutes

Materials and space required

Students play in groups of 2 to 5. Each group needs a table for the game board and chairs to sit around the table.

Below is one suggestion for the board, but this game works best if the students create their own board.

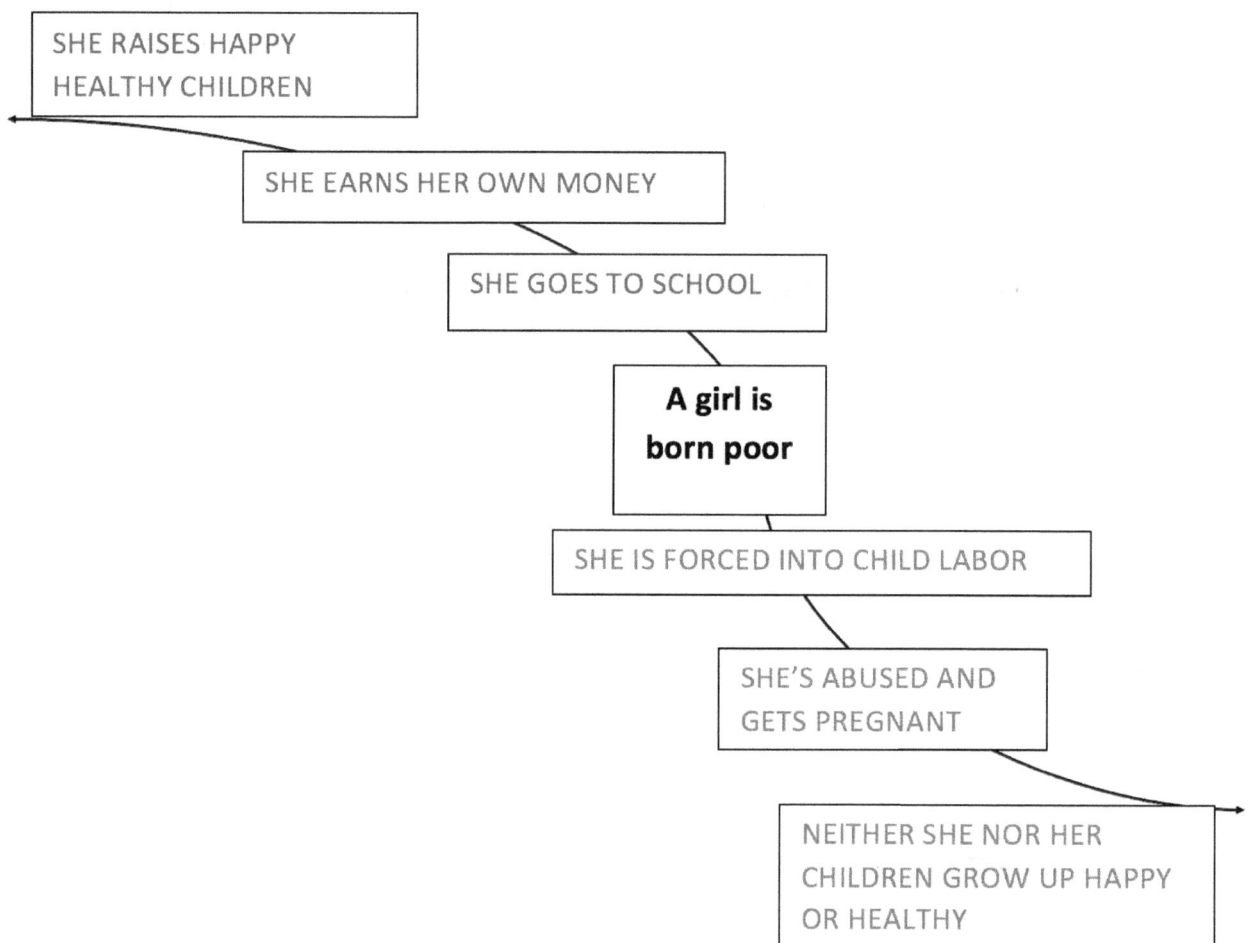

SHE RAISES HAPPY
HEALTHY CHILDREN

SHE EARNS HER OWN MONEY

SHE GOES TO SCHOOL

**A girl is
born poor**

SHE IS FORCED INTO CHILD LABOR

SHE'S ABUSED AND
GETS PREGNANT

NEITHER SHE NOR HER
CHILDREN GROW UP HAPPY
OR HEALTHY

Instructions

Before the game: Students watch the video of the "Girl Effect" (youtube.com/watch?v=1e8xgF0JtVg) two or three times. They note down what information surprised them.

This game works best if the students imagine two complete stories: one a positive story about a girl and the other negative. They write the elements of the story on cards and create their own board. There should be a neutral card in the center that suggests a situation, for example: a girl is born poor. Then there should be an equal number of cards, ideally either 6 or 12 leading in opposite directions from the center card.

T₁H₄E₁ G₂A₁M₃E₁

Players start on the middle card, in this case on the card which says "A girl is born poor."

The first player flips a coin to determine which direction to go. Then the same player rolls the dice (one or two dice depending on how many cards there) are to see how many spaces to go.

Then the second player takes their turn in the same way. The participants continue playing until each player has reached either the positive end or the negative end.

If the players have created their own game boards, the players can repeat the game using the different boards.

Follow-up tasks

Speaking: The students play similar games with other contexts, for example:

An inner-city boy who might become involved in a street gang.

Some of the cards might look like this:

POSITIVE ENDING		STARTING POSITION CARD		NEGATIVE ENDING
He graduates, gets a job and moves away from the neighborhood.	He chooses not to pursue the friendship.	He makes friends with a known gang member.	He is initiated into the gang.	He gets into a fight and dies.

A boy in a war-torn country who may be recruited into terrorism.

The cards might look like this:

POSITIVE ENDING		STARTING POSITION CARD		NEGATIVE ENDING
He teaches his children to promote peace and tolerance.	He goes to school and is taught that his religion promotes love.	He is born in a country torn by war.	A terrorist organization recruits and brainwashes him. He believes God wants him to kill.	He becomes a suicide bomber.

A young person who may be lured by drugs.

The cards might look like this:

POSITIVE ENDING She leads a healthy and successful life.	She chooses not to do drugs again.	STARTING POSITION CARD A teenager tries drugs for the first time at a party.	She enjoys her first experience with drugs and develops a habit.	NEGATIVE ENDING She dies of an overdose.

A child who is unable to delay gratification.

The cards might look like this:

POSITIVE ENDING She successfully graduates while maintaining a happy social life	She chooses to do her homework but arranges a play date for the weekend.	STARTING POSITION CARD A child gets homework from her school teacher but her friends have invited her to play	She chooses to go out and forgets to complete her homework. She gets a failing mark	NEGATIVE ENDING She fails school repeatedly until she drops out

Writing: Students can write their thoughts about these games in a journal.

Students can also write a "choose your own adventure"-type of story, based on what they have learned from these games by following the steps in Game 14.

GAME 17

HOME TEAM

Why play the game

In the United States, poor children often idolize basketball and American football players who have made it out of poverty, while in Canada they dream of playing professional hockey. In Latin America, Europe and Africa, many children have a similar dream of becoming football players as a way out of poverty to fame and fortune. In all of these cases, there can be many obstacles to success. To begin with, the chances of having the talent necessary to be chosen to play in the "big leagues" is slim. Then, training for such a career often precludes the chance to work for anything else, which means that if that dream is shattered, there may be little else to replace it.

Game objective

To show how fragile the dream of a successful athletic career is

End point of the game

The winners are those who continue playing until they win the championship. The game should refer to whichever sport is most important in the students' lives. If the career is professional soccer, then the aim is to win the World Cup, if hockey, the Stanley Cup, if baseball, the World Series, etc.

Type of game

Physical

Number of players

Unlimited

Level/age of players

Beginner and up, teenagers and up

Preparation time

The teacher will need to prepare the following cards ahead of time. These cards have been written to reflect the life of a soccer player, but the cards can be adapted to any sport. (downloadable/photocopiable version found at http://wayzgoosepress.com/wp-content/uploads/2016/09/Social-Change-Game-17.pdf)

You have been spotted by a talent scout.	**You have made the national team.**
You have to quit school to train full time.	**You got caught using drugs and you've been kicked off the team.**
You've been traded to an English team.	**You have won the World Cup.**
You will have to leave your family behind to train full time. You won't see your children.	**You've broken your leg and can never play again.**

Playing time

5 to 20 minutes, depending on the number of students

Materials and space required

An outdoor space where a ball can be safely kicked into a goal

Instructions

Before the game: Students find and share stories of famous athletes who overcame obstacles to achieve fame and success. They listen to each other's stories and note similarities and differences.

THE GAME

Players take turns trying to score a goal, with the teacher or a volunteer student as goalie. If the player fails to score a goal, they are "out". If the player scores, they are randomly given a card with good or bad news. If the news is good, the player continues playing, but if the news is bad, they are eliminated.

The game continues with remaining players taking turns until there is only one player left.

Follow-up tasks

Speaking: Students work in pairs to role play the following scene:

> Teenager: You are a young athlete and your coach has told you that you are extremely talented. You try to convince your parents to let you drop out of school to train full-time.

> Parent: Your child is a talented athlete and you want to be encouraging, but you don't think dropping out of school is a good idea.

Writing: Students write a story about an imaginary young athlete. The story should have at least four different possible endings, only one of which would be a life of fame and fortune. They then read their stories aloud to classmates asking them to choose their paths through the story as in Game 14.

GAME 18

PAPARAZZI

Why play the game

"Paparazzi" refers to photographers who pursue celebrities to get photographs of them. However, often they don't only pursue actors or athletes, but also common people who find themselves in the media spotlight for whatever reason. A danger is when ordinary people, especially young people, find that people have taken photos of them and posted them on social media such as Facebook or Instagram. Sometimes these photos can put them in a difficult position. For example, supposing they go to a party, and the next day their employers or family members see photos of them drunk or in compromising positions.

The aim of this game is for students to both pursue and be pursued as photographers and "victims." This requires them to be vigilant so they can take as many pictures as possible of others while having as few as possible taken of them. It also makes a very good activity for the first week of classes at a university where the students all move around on the same campus but may not know each other by sight.

The game works best if every student has a camera, or one on their cellphone. It works even better if you have set up a private class Facebook page so that they can post their photos, but if you haven't done that, they can simply mingle the next day in class showing each other their photos.

Game objective

The aim of this game is for students to both pursue and be pursued as photographers and "victims."

End point of the game

One winner is the player who has taken the most photos of classmates. The second winner is the player who has evaded the photographers and has had the fewest photos taken of him or her.

Type of game

Photography

Number of players

Unlimited

Level/age of players

Beginner and up, teenagers and up

Preparation time

None

Playing time

23 hours, or the time between one class meeting and the next

Materials and space required

Camera or cellphone camera for each player

Instructions

Before the game: Students find out the meaning of the term *paparazzi*. Then the teacher plays the song "Piece of Me" by Britney Spears (youtube.com/watch?v=u4FF6MpcsRw). The class may listen to it two or three times in order to answer the following question: *Why is the singer angry at the media?*

THE GAME

Players have from the end of one class to the beginning of the next one to take as many candid photos of their classmates as possible while avoiding being photographed themselves.

Follow-up tasks

Speaking: The students prepare presentations and posters about internet privacy and the potential dangers of social media. They can then present to other groups, or even local elementary and high schools.

Writing: If the students have posted the photos on the class Facebook page, they can then comment on the photos. It becomes more interesting when they are encouraged to make up stories about what the person was doing in the photograph. For example, a student looking through her backpack may find themselves the subject of a story involving selling illegal drugs. Interestingly, the stories will be more creative the more restrictions the teacher places, such as requiring the students to use certain grammar points or vocabulary.

GAME 19

P A R T Y

Why play the game

Peer pressure can lead young people to drink or do drugs they otherwise might not.

Game objective

To become aware of the consequences of the abuse of alcohol or non-prescription drugs

End point of the game

To choose the best path through the story

Type of game

This is similar to the "choose your path" videos shown at teens.drugabuse.gov/peerx/choose-your-path.

Number of players

Unlimited although players will make their videos in small groups

Level/age of players

Intermediate and up, teenagers and up

Preparation time

Several classes to prepare their videos

Playing time

5 to 15 minutes per video

Materials and space required

Cellphone video cameras and any props chosen by the players for their video. Each player also needs pen and paper.

Instructions

Before the game: Students watch the "choose your path" videos shown at teens.drugabuse.gov/peerx/choose-your-path. As they are watching, they should vote on the choices offered. They can watch the videos as many times as they want in order to see all of the options played out.

Students film a story about a person consuming too much alcohol, and the consequences of this activity. Each story should have multiple endings.

Having made the videos of each of the different parts of the story, the students upload the different parts of the story to an online video service, such as YouTube or Vimeo. Each video has links to the options for the continuation of the story.

THE GAME

Each group presents their videos to the class. After each segment, the class votes on which segment to see next.

Follow-up tasks

Speaking: Students roleplay the following situation:

Student 1: You are at a party. You do not want to drink, but you do want to join in the fun with your friends.

Student 2: You are at a party. You think your friend is being too serious. You offer your friend a drink to relax.

Writing: The students combine the stories they heard to write an essay or create a poster on the dangers of drinking; they can donate these to local high schools or post them in their own classroom or school.

GAME 20

P O O R

E C O N O M I C S

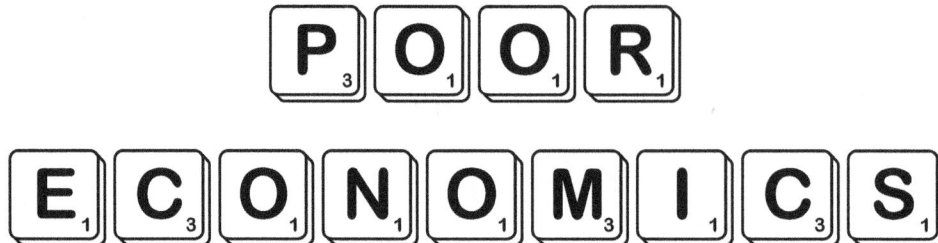

Why play the game

Many people assume that poverty is the result of laziness. On the other end of the spectrum, other people believe that poverty exists simply because the rich are not generous enough. Esther Duflo and Abhijit Banerjee have made it their life's work to find out the real causes of poverty at the grassroots level.

This game is based on the book *Poor Economics: A Radical Rethinking of the Way to Fight Global Poverty* (Duflo & Banerjee, 2011), as well as a MIT MOOC (mooc-list.com/course/1473x-challenges-global-poverty-edx) taught by the authors. The aim is to have students understand that the reasons that people are poor are not always the most obvious ones, and that this understanding can arm us with better tools to fight poverty. The true/false statements in the game all reflect some aspect explained in the book or on the course.

Game objective

To be aware of the living conditions experience by people who live in extreme poverty, and to understand the reasons for the choices they make

End point of the game

The winner is the team with the most correct answers.

Type of game

True or false questions

Number of players

Unlimited

Level/age of players

Teenagers and up, intermediate and up

Preparation time

The teacher prints out the following statements ahead of time. The answers and explanations are given below.

1. The poorer they are, the hungrier they are; thus, the more money they get, the more they will spend on calories.

2. The heavier the subsidy on rice, the more they buy.

3. The better a child is fed, the more they will earn as an adult.

4. The poorer the people are, the less they spend on weddings and funerals.

5. The cheaper the medicine, the more likely people are to take it.

6. The poorer the country, the more likely people are to get malaria.

7. The poorer the patients, the more likely they are to go to a private doctor.

8. The less qualified the doctors, the more likely they are to prescribe medicine.

9. The more people believe in shaman medicine, the less they believe in conventional medicine.

10. The more children people have, the more likely only the oldest will go to school.

11. The more you go to school, the more you will learn.

12. The poorer the parents, the less likely the children will go to school.

13. The lower the child's self-esteem, the less well they will do in school.

14. The better trained the teachers are, the better the education they will provide.

15. The more teenage girls are educated about HIV, the less likely they are to have sex.

16. The more school uniforms are given out for free, the fewer the number of teenage pregnancies.

17. The more telenovelas women watch, the fewer children they will have.

18. The easier the access to contraceptives, the lower the fertility rate.

Answers and explanations:

1. False. Rather than buying a high-calorie food such as rice, more will use extra money to buy "treats," like tea or shrimp.

2. False. They will use the extra money to buy something else, unless they are truly starving.

3. True. This applies not only to overall calories consumed, but also to micronutrients necessary for better health and brain development.

4. False. Weddings and funerals are often important events in a family, and they will often save up for years to celebrate (or mourn) in a style calculated to impress their neighbors or pay proper tribute.

5. False. The cheapest medicine is usually to prevent disease in the first place, yet the poor often do not have their children vaccinated, chlorinate their drinking water, or use mosquito nets.

6. Unknown. Places like Colombia and Ecuador control malaria well, while thousands in Africa die of it. It is unknown what government policies or cultural practices are responsible for this discrepancy.

7. True. People have an abiding belief that "you get what you pay for." This means that many people, even the poorest, would prefer to go to a private doctor, all else being equal.

8. True. Many doctors in the poorest areas barely even have a high school diploma. These doctors may believe it is better for their reputation and prestige to give the wrong medicine than none at all.

9. False. Many people are willing to use whichever kind of medicine they believe will work best.

10. False. If forced to choose, parents will usually send the child they believe is the smartest to school, who may or may not be the oldest.

11. False. School teachers are often only barely more educated than their students. In addition, difficult teaching conditions, poor infrastructure and other problems often lead to teacher and student absenteeism.

12. True. Even though schools may be free, uniforms and books rarely are. In addition, many of the extreme poor need their children at home to help the family to earn money.

13. True. If children believe that they cannot learn because of their gender, race, background or other factors, this becomes a self-fulfilling prophecy.

14. False. Education depends as much on materials, infrastructure, and culture as on teacher quality; there is often only so much a good teacher can do to counter other obstacles.

15. True. Poor teenage girls rarely have sex for pleasure. Statistically, they are more likely to sleep with an older man in the hopes that he will marry her, allowing her to escape her family's poverty. When the girls learn that older men are more likely to carry HIV, they will choose to avoid them.

16. True. Often a girl's school uniform is the prettiest item of clothing she owns and she is proud to wear it. Therefore, she will stay in school.

17. True. In a study done in Brazil, where researchers were able to compare villages where people had televisions with equally poor villages which did not, they noticed that women who watch telenovelas had seen that many characters had few children.

18. In Catholic or other religious cultures, even if birth control is freely available, many women will choose not to use it.

Playing time

30 minutes

Materials and space required

A classroom. Each player needs pen and paper.

Instructions

Before the game: The teacher posts the following arguments on opposite sides of the room.

Some people believe that the poor are extremely lazy. They have received charity from countries and individuals but have not used it wisely. There is no point in continuing to help.

Some people argue that it takes so little to help the poor that we are morally obliged to give what we can. For example, it doesn't cost much to buy vitamins or vaccinations for a child, so we should help.

The students position themselves physically at the point between the two statements they feel bests represents their opinion.

T͟H͟E͟ G͟A͟M͟E͟

Players are divided into two teams. The teacher reads the statements aloud to them. Each team take turns to decide which statements are true and which are false.

Follow-up tasks

Speaking: Students discuss their thoughts after this game, noting particularly what points surprised them. They then find out how the original study was done; advanced students might critique the research methods.

Writing: Students can plan an education campaign for the poor in their community; for example, encouraging them to vaccinate their children, or teaching them proper nutrition. They must make sure that they are respectful in their campaign and that they do not come across as offensive in any way. Then they decide how best to disseminate their campaign.

GAME 21

POVERTY

BLACKJACK

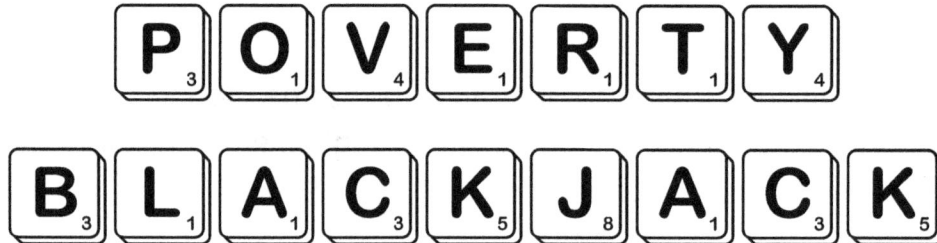

Why play the game

Nearly one billion people live on less than $2 a day. It may be hard for some people to imagine how little that really is.

Game objective

To realize the limited buying power of $2 (or local equivalent) a day

End point of the game

To buy as much as possible without exceeding the $2 limit

Type of game

This game is similar to blackjack. In blackjack, the aim is to get as close to 21 points as possible without going over. In this game, the aim is to buy as much as you can, but you don't have more than two dollars to spend.

Number of players

Unlimited

Level/age of players

Teenagers and up, intermediate and up

Preparation time

Instead of regular cards, the game is played with special cards with pictures of everyday items (for example, French fries), with their price. There are some examples below, but students will need time to make their own cards.

$0.65

$1.50

$0.50

Playing time

20 to 40 minutes

Materials and space required

The cards and a table, seating arrangements for groups of 3-6 players.

Instructions

Before the game: Students make cards: on each card, they draw something they buy every day, along with the price. They can use the cards pictured above as examples.

T H E   G A M E

One student is the dealer, and deals each of the players one card face down. The players (but not the dealer) may look at the cards. The dealer also deals one card face up, including one for the dealer. The dealer then distributes as many cards as each player asks for, until the player is either as close to $2.00 as possible or has gone over. The winner is whoever has closest to $2.00 without going over.

Follow-up tasks

Writing: Students can attempt to live for a day on less than $2 (or the local equivalent) and then write in their journals about the experience. It might be useful for each student to calculate how much money they usually spend on an average day. Whatever they haven't spent can be donated to a charity of the students' choice; for example, if they usually spend $10.00, and on this day they spend $2.00, they can donate $8.00.

Speaking: In order to choose the charity, each student, or group of students research a charity that they present to the class. After the presentations, the students vote on the charity they will all donate to.

GAME 22

P R O T E S T   A R T

Why play the game

Protest art has a long history, covering everything from commissioned oil paintings to street graffiti. It usually shows images or symbols juxtaposed in such a way as to make the viewer stop and think about the message. Students may want to look at websites featuring the artwork of Banksy or they can look at the site at ca.complex.com/style/2013/07/new-political-art/vik-muniz, showing interesting protest art works.

This is another game from which the maximum benefits come when the students design the material themselves. It provides an opportunity for the students to search online for art that is meaningful to them, and to consider why and how it affects them.

Game objective

To analyze protest art

End point of the game

The first team to match all of their descriptions to the art correctly wins.

Type of game

Matching

Number of players

Unlimited

Level/age of players

Teenagers and up, intermediate and up

Preparation time

1 to 2 classes for the players to select the art and prepare the cards

Playing time

20 to 30 minutes

Materials and space required

A space where the art may be placed on walls or tables around the room

Instructions

Before the game: Players are divided into two (or more) teams. Each team finds ten different works of protest art, which they can find online or in print. For each work of art, they write a short description and explanation on a card. The students can include specific grammar or vocabulary, according to the teacher's instructions.

THE GAME

The teams put their art on the walls of the classroom. They hand another team the cards containing the descriptions. The first team to match all of their descriptions to the works of art correctly wins.

Follow-up tasks

Speaking: Students discuss their favorite pieces of art from this project.

Writing: Students research and write an essay on the meaning of a work of art chosen by a classmate. The classmate then reads and responds to the essay by noting what new or surprising information they learned.

GAME 23

QUEST OF A SLAVE WOMAN

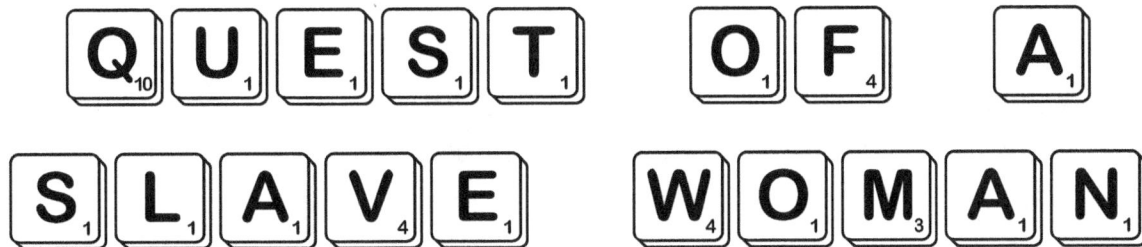

Why play the game

The United States used African-Americans as slaves for nearly 100 years.

Imagine what it would be like to be a slave. Really imagine it. You have no freedom. You have no possessions. Even the children you give birth to are not your own. They can be taken from you at any time.

In *Incidents in the Life of a Slave Girl*, Harriet Jacobs (spartacus-educational.com/Sjacobs.htm) tells this story:

> On one of these sale days, I saw a mother lead seven children to the auction-block. She knew that some of them would be taken from her; but they took all. The children were sold to a slave-trader, and their mother was bought by a man in her own town. Before night her children were all far away. She begged the trader to tell her where he x to take them; this he refused to do. How could he, when he knew he would sell them, one by one, wherever he could command the highest price? I met that mother in the street, and her wild, haggard face lives to-day in my mind. She wrung her hands in anguish, and exclaimed, Gone! All gone! Why don't God kill me? I had no words wherewith to comfort her. Instances of this kind are of daily, yea, of hourly occurrence. (Jacobs, 1861, p. 17)

Slaves, of course, may not learn to read or write, for the written word is freedom. Many African-American slaves, however, learned in secret and wrote shocking accounts of their tragic lives.

Many Caucasians, though not nearly enough, were adamantly opposed to slavery. Feminists, in particular, saw parallels between the fact that both women and slaves were treated as property and denied basic rights such as universal suffrage.

John Simkins compiled an encyclopedia (spartacus-educational.com/USAslavery.htm) of facts about slavery based on documents, texts, narratives and personal accounts written during that period.

The slave narratives speak for themselves. They are shocking in their honesty and in the brutal conditions they reveal. These are not stories that may simply be read for pleasure. They show the ugly side of American national history and the potential evil of all human beings in their ability to dehumanize one another and cause unimaginable pain and suffering.

Game objective

To interact with the narratives and information in the Simkins encyclopedia in character

End point of the game

Either the escaped slave finds out what happened to her children and escapes, or the bounty hunter captures her and her children.

Type of game

Quest, role play

Number of players

Students play in pairs

Level/age of players

Adults, advanced English level

Preparation time

None

Playing time

Approximately 30-40 minutes

Materials and space required

Players sit in pairs, but each player needs internet access on separate devices. They each need pen and paper placed so that each can read the other's notes. They also need one die per pair.

Instructions

Before the game: Introduce the issue of slavery by showing students a video of *capoeira angola* such as the one at youtube.com/watch?v=_gPi78MfVG4, and a video of *karate* such as youtube.com/watch?v=os6AKhus2pg. Students create a Venn diagram comparing and contrasting the two. (Note to teacher: both are martial arts, but *capoeira* is more dance like and set to music because it was performed by Brazilian slaves who did not wish their masters to realize that they were, in fact, not dancing, but training to rebel. The movements are slower in *capoeira angola* and legs are generally kept close together, unlike the high kicks performed in *karate*, because many slaves wore chains on their ankles.) Students may follow up by considering and discussing what it might mean to be a slave.

The teacher reads the text by Harriet Jacobs above and students respond in their journals.

T·H·E G·A·M·E

The teacher introduces the game by explaining the following:

The aim of this game is to have the readers *interact* with the texts rather than just reading their words. The game is designed, therefore, to have the writers of the different narratives act as NPCs (non-player characters) in the slave woman's quest to find her four children who were sold away from her.

One player is the **SLAVE WOMAN** who must follow clues to find her children. The clues are given as hyperlinks to the narratives and documents in the encyclopedia. She will write about what she finds out and post the information in a public place for all of the other slaves to read (in this case, Facebook or Twitter). However, she may change a few of the details, because she knows she is being followed by a bounty hunter who wants to capture her and she wants to throw him off the scent.

The other player is the **BOUNTY HUNTER** who is trying to capture the slave, but is waiting to see if she will lead him to her four children as well, because then he will have five healthy adults to sell. He will also follow the (hyperlinked) clues, and he is also obligated to post what he finds out for his investors. However, he realizes the slave woman can read and so he, too, will change some of the details so that she doesn't find her children before he does.

In order to create the hunter-hunted experience in the game, the players throw dice every five-minute interval. If they roll the same number, the hunter will capture the slave and sell her at auction.

The teacher provides the following cards to the players; they begin the game (downloadable/photocopiable version found at http://wayzgoosepress.com/wp-content/uploads/2016/09/Social-Change-Game-23.pdf).

SLAVE WOMAN

You are an escaped slave. A bounty hunter is trying to find you.

Roll the dice with the bounty hunter; if you get the same number, he will catch you and drag you back to the plantation where you will be punished. If this happens twice, the second time you will be executed. If you roll different numbers, pick up the next card and continue.

You have two goals:

1. Find out what happened to your four children who were sold from you about 10 years ago. You need to find them before the bounty hunter does.

2. Take notes for an autobiography you want to write to expose the injustice and cruelty of the slave system. **Start by describing your life as a house slave** (spartacus-educational.com/USASdomestic.htm). **Note it on the paper.**

Note: Be aware that the bounty hunter might read what you write: it's important to tell the truth but you might want to change some details to throw him off. Also, you do not have time to write very much, maximum 100 words per note.

You think one of your daughters may have died as a field slave.

Ask Mary Prince (spartacus-educational.com/SprinceM.htm) **OR Henry Box Brown** (spartacus-educational.com/USASbox.htm) **how slaves usually die on plantations. Note it on the paper.**

Roll the dice; if you are not captured you may continue to search for your other three children.

You've heard of the Underground Railroad. You aren't quite sure what it is, but you have information that one of your sons may have escaped north that way.

Ask Harriet Tubman (spartacus-educational.com/USAStubman.htm) **OR Sojourner Truth** (spartacus-educational.com/USAStruth.htm) **how slaves escaped on the Underground Railroad. Note it on the paper.**

Roll the dice; if you are not captured you may continue to search for your other two children.

Some slaves revolted. You think one of your sons may have participated in one.

Ask Nat Turner (spartacus-educational.com/USASturner.htm) **or Frederick Douglass** (spartacus-educational.com/USASdouglass.htm) **what happened to most slaves involved in rebellions. Note it on the paper.**

Roll the dice; if you are not captured you may continue to search for your last child.

You know that your youngest daughter has found sympathetic white friends.

Ask Angelina Grimke (spartacus-educational.com/USASgrimke.htm) **OR Harriet Beecher Stowe** (spartacus-educational.com/USASstowe.htm) **if the suffragettes would have helped her. Note it on the paper.**

Roll the dice; if you are not captured you may continue and check your answers.

THE ANSWERS: Slave Woman

Your first daughter probably died from a whipping.

The second child, your son, probably escaped along with hundreds of others along the Underground Railway to the North and to freedom.

Your third son was probably executed after participating in a rebellion.

Your youngest daughter is probably alive and working for pay in the household of one of the suffragettes.

You have lost two children, but your two living children are safe and cannot be captured by the bounty hunter.

Roll the dice one last time. If you escape you may go free.

BOUNTY HUNTER

You are a bounty hunter. You are chasing an escaped slave.

Roll the dice with the slave; if you get the same number, you can catch her and drag her back to the plantation where she will be punished. If this happens twice, the second time she will be executed. If you roll different numbers, pick up the next card and continue.

You have two goals:

1. Capture the slave, but ideally, you also want to capture her children whom you know were sold away at auction about 10 years ago. You need to find them before the slave does.

2. Keep notes of what you find out for the investors who are supporting you.

Start by explaining the laws that allow you to catch runaway slaves (spartacus-educational.com/USASfugitive.htm). **Note it on the paper.**

Note: Be aware that the slave might read what you write: it's important to tell the truth but you might want to change some details to throw her off. Also, you do not have time to write very much, maximum 100 words per note.

You think one of her daughters may have died as a field slave.

Ask Moses Grandy (spartacus-educational.com/USASgrandy.htm) **OR Elizabeth Keckley** (spartacus-educational.com/USASkeckley.htm) **how slaves usually die on plantations. Note it on the paper.**

Roll the dice; if you do not capture the slave you may continue to search for her other three children.

You've heard of the Underground Railroad. You aren't quite sure what it is, but you have information that one of the slave's sons may have escaped north that way.

Ask Harriet Tubman (spartacus-educational.com/USAStubman.htm) **OR Sojourner Truth**(spartacus-educational.com/USAStruth.htm) **how slaves escaped on the Underground Railroad. Note it on the paper.**

Roll the dice; if you do not capture the slave you may continue to search for her other two children.

Some slaves revolted. You think one of her sons may have participated in one.

Ask Nat Turner (spartacus-educational.com/USASturner.htm) **or Frederick Douglass** (spartacus-educational.com/USASdouglass.htm) **what happened to most slaves involved in rebellions. Note it on the paper.**

Roll the dice; if you do not capture the slave you may continue to search for her last child.

You know that your youngest daughter has found sympathetic white friends.

Ask Angelina Grimke(spartacus-educational.com/USASgrimke.htm) **OR Harriet Beecher Stowe** (spartacus-educational.com/USASstowe.htm) **if the suffragettes would have helped her. Note it on the paper.**

Roll the dice; if you do not capture the slave you may continue and check your answers.

THE ANSWERS: Bounty Hunter

Her first daughter probably died from a whipping.

The second child, her son, probably escaped along with hundreds of others along the Underground Railway to the North and to freedom.

Her third son was probably executed after participating in a rebellion.

Her youngest daughter is probably alive and working for pay in the household of one of the suffragettes.

You cannot capture any of the slave's children and your investors have pulled out.

Roll the dice one last time. If you do not capture her, leave her alone and pursue someone else.

Follow-up tasks

Writing: Players who played the role of the slave woman conclude the game by writing what she has learned from her experience. She wants to leave this document as a testament to the cruelty and injustice of slavery in the hopes that it will be abolished.

Players who played the role of the bounty hunter must write up a report of the events in the game for the boss who financed them.

Speaking: Students discuss the following questions, first in pairs, then as a class:

a) Slavery was an economic system that permitted the rapid development of the United States (and other countries). Other than the fact that slavery is immoral, what arguments were used to persuade the people in power to stop using slavery as the foundation of that economic system?

b) What remains to be done in the fight for racial equality today?

GAME 24

S₁ T₁ R₁ E₁ E₁ T₁   V₄ A₁ L₁ U₁ E₁ S₁

Why play the game

People who live on the streets often have different values than others might. This game is meant to highlight how ethics and values come from the circumstances in which we live.

Game objective

To evaluate events from a different point of view

End point of the game

To compare scores with others and discuss why they are different

Type of game

Discussion

Number of players

Unlimited but students play in pairs

Level/age of players

Teenagers and older, level intermediate and higher

Preparation time

5 minutes to print and cut the cards and to lay them face down on a table

Playing time

20 to 30 minutes

Materials and space required

One set of cards placed face down on a table at the front of the room. Players should sit in pairs, and note the scores they agree on.

Instructions

Before the game: The students listen to the following songs in three different groups, and then compare and contrast the songs. They can consider the following questions:

Who is the singer talking about and how old is this person/how old are these people?

What suggestions does the singer have?

- Group 1 listens to "Cardboard Box City" by the Levellers (youtube. com/watch?v=UfWtmCpByYc).
- Group 2 listens to "Rosemary" by Lenny Kravitz (youtube.com/ watch?v=Jb-55iYTUts).
- Group 3 listens to "Nobody's Home" by Avril Lavigne (youtube. com/watch?v=NGFSNE18Ywc).

T H E   G A M E

Players take turns choosing a card from the main table, bringing it back to their seats, and deciding if the event described is a happy one or an unhappy one from the point of view of a homeless child using the following scale:

$$-3 \mid -2 \mid -1 \mid 0 \mid +1 \mid +2 \mid +3$$

They then return the card to the main table and select another, until they have discussed all of the cards (downloadable/photocopiable version found at http://wayzgoosepress. com/wp-content/uploads/2016/09/Social-Change-Game-24.pdf).

I FOUND AN OLD FOOTBALL. WE PLAYED FOR AN HOUR. WE WON!

SOMEONE DROPPED A CELL PHONE. I SOLD IT TO A GUY FOR $25.

I SAT OUTSIDE A BAKERY. A RICH TOURIST BOUGHT ME A CHOCOLATE CAKE.

I FELL FACE DOWN IN MUD. EVERYONE LAUGHED AT ME.

I WAS COLD, SO I SLEPT IN A DOG HOUSE IN A RICH NEIGHBORHOOD.

I WATCHED A MOVIE THROUGH THE WINDOW OF AN ELECTRONICS STORE.

BIG KID JOE BEAT ME UP.

GUARDS THREW ME OUT OF THE MALL. I'M COLD.

BIG KID JOE STOLE AN OLD LADY'S PURSE. SHE THOUGHT I DID IT, SO I HAD TO RUN.

```
+---------------------------------------------------------------+
|                  A DOG TREED ME FOR 2 HOURS.                  |
+---------------------------------------------------------------+
| I WAS LOOKING IN A CAR WINDOW, AND A COP HIT ME ON THE HEAD WITH HIS NIGHTSTICK. |
+---------------------------------------------------------------+
|    I WON A CONTEST WITH A CAB DRIVER TO SEE WHO COULD SPIT FARTHEST.    |
|                                                               |
|                  HE BOUGHT ME A HAMBURGER.                    |
+---------------------------------------------------------------+
|    I SAW A DRUNK SLEEPING IN THE PARK, AND I STOLE HIS JACKET AND HAT.    |
+---------------------------------------------------------------+
|    I PASSED A SCHOOL WHERE KIDS WERE WEARING NICE CLOTHES. I HATE THEM.    |
+---------------------------------------------------------------+
|    I STOOD OUTSIDE A RESTAURANT LOOKING IN. I'VE NEVER HAD ICE CREAM BEFORE.    |
+---------------------------------------------------------------+
|    I STOLE A COLA FROM A STORE. I OPENED THE CAP AND WON A FREE ONE.    |
+---------------------------------------------------------------+
|    I WON $4 FROM BIG KID JOE BECAUSE MY FOOTBALL TEAM BEAT HIS.    |
+---------------------------------------------------------------+
```

Players add up their score and discuss any differences.

Follow-up tasks

Speaking: Players add up their score and discuss any differences.

Writing: The students imagine a day in the life of a homeless child. After they've written out a story, they each read another student's story and find good illustrations for it.

GAME 25

STRING OF PEARLS

Why play the game

Jesse Schell suggested that good storytelling in video games is often achieved this way:

> The idea is that a completely non-interactive story (the string) is presented in the form of text, a slideshow, or an animated sequence and then the player is given a period of free movement and control (the pearl) with a fixed goal in mind. When the goal is achieved, the player travels down the string via another non-interactive sequence, to the next pearl, etc. In other words, cut scene, game level, cut scene, game level….
>
> Many people criticize this method as "not really being interactive," but players sure do enjoy it. (Schell, 2015, p. 299)

Game objective

To surprise the listener through telling a story

End point of the game

The conclusion of the story

Type of game

Storytelling

Number of players

Unlimited but players play in pairs

Level/age of players

Teenagers and older, teachers, levels intermediate and up

Preparation time

Approximately 1 to 2 weeks for the players to prepare.

Playing time

20 to 60 minutes

Materials and space required

Comfortable seating in pairs

Instructions

Before the game: Each player reads a short story or watches a movie, and then prepares a summary and questions. It works best if the story has a surprise ending or unusual plot twists, particularly if the characters are deep and interesting. The questions may include the following types:

- Predictive: for example, What do you think will happen next?
- Descriptive: for example, What kind of person is this character?
- Opinion: for example, Do you like this character?
- Hypothetical: for example, What do you think this character might do if the situation were reversed?
- Imaginary: for example, What was this character's childhood like?
- Counterfactual: for example, What would have happened if the character hadn't done this?

THE GAME

Player A faces Player B and begins to tell the story they have prepared. At a specified number of crucial points in the story, Player A stops to ask Player B questions. When they get to the end of Player A's story, they switch roles.

Follow-up tasks

Speaking: Players describe how they felt about the story. In particular, they note which plot twists or character elements surprised them most and why.

Players find similarities and differences between the characters in their stories.

Players further delve into the characters by discussing questions such as these found in *The Book of Questions* by Gregory Stock from the character's point of view:

1. For a person you loved deeply, would you be willing to move to a distant country knowing there would be little chance of seeing your friends or family again?

2. Do you believe in ghosts or evil spirits? Would you be willing to spend a night alone in a remote house that is supposedly haunted?

3. If you were to die this evening with no opportunity to communicate with anyone, what would you most regret not having told someone? Why haven't you told them yet?

4. If you could spend one year in prefect happiness but afterward would remember nothing of the experience would you do so? If not, Why not? 4b: Which is more important: actual experiences, or the memories that remain when the experiences are over?

5. If a new medicine were developed that would cure arthritis but cause a fatal reaction in one percent of those who took it, would you want it to be released to the public?

6. You discover your wonderful one-year-old child is, because of a mix up at the hospital, not yours. Would you want to exchange the child to try to correct the mistake?

Writing: Students compare the characters to themselves.

GAME 26

T E A C H I N G
V A L U E S

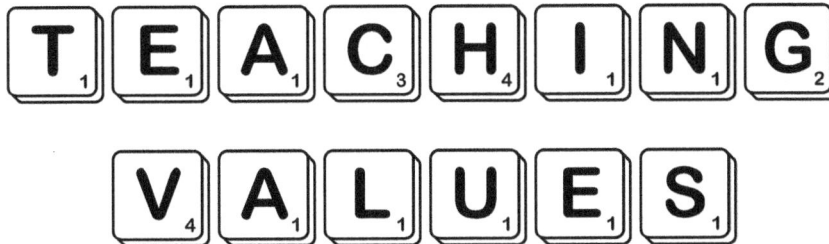

Why play the game

If we really believe in teaching honesty and other values such as collaboration, empathy, honor, respect, and inclusion, then we need to reassess our way of teaching. Rewards and punishments will only go so far in teaching what really needs to be taught.

Game objective

To solve classroom problems

End point of the game

To agree on a class constitution

Type of game

Card, discussion

Number of players

5 to 10

Level/age of players

Teenagers and older, teachers, levels intermediate and up

Preparation time

None

Playing time

30-60 minutes

Materials and space required

Players need pen and paper. They work in pairs for steps 1, 2, and 3, and then move the seats into a circle for the remaining steps.

Instructions

Before the game: Players individually write a list of as many of their values (for example, honesty, effort…) as possible in 100 seconds. They then put that list aside, but keep it handy.

Players individually write a list of 5-8 common classroom problems (for example, copying/giving a zero, using cellphones during class/removing them), along with their ideas for solutions.

Players look at all of their solution cards. Then, they decide which ones describe a reward or a punishment. They must eliminate the ones that describe a reward or a punishment, and then think of other solutions (for example, copying vs. giving assignments that are creative and cannot be copied, using cellphones vs. taking advantage of the fact that they have cellphones to create an internet quest).

T H E   G A M E

The cards are laid out face down with all of the problems on one side of the table and all of the solutions on the other.

The first player selects a pair of cards so that they have one problem with its corresponding solution. The player can keep the pair only if they can prove that the solution teaches students at least three of the values on their list. Otherwise, the player puts the pair of cards face down on the table and the game continues with the next player.

The game continues until all of the problems have been given solutions.

Follow-up tasks

Speaking: Based on the ideas from this game, agree on a class constitution with the rights and duties of the students and the teachers.

Writing: Students commit to the constitution by means of a written pledge, which they must sign. If they wish, they may include any objections, which they may bring up for the class to discuss.

GAME 27

TOXIC LOVE

Why play the game

Many young people are in psychologically, sexually, physically, or financially abusive romantic relationships. Most do not realize that they are being mistreated because there is an aura of secrecy around what goes on. They don't tell anyone what's happening because on the one hand, they blame themselves and are ashamed, yet on the other, they think it's normal. For example, if a boy constantly mocks his girlfriend's body shape, she may feel ashamed, yet not recognize this as a form of emotional abuse. At a more extreme level, partners may pressure each other into sexual activity for which they aren't ready as "proof of their love."

Game objective

To discuss healthy and unhealthy behavior in a romantic relationship

End point of the game

One team wins by giving the most answers that agree with the survey results.

Type of game

Survey

Number of players

10 to 30 players

Level/age of players

Teenagers and older, intermediate and higher

Preparation time

1 to 2 class periods

Playing time

20 to 30 minutes

Materials and space required

Classroom with desks and chairs, pens, paper, board markers, whiteboard

Instructions

Before the game: Students work in pairs to prepare yes/no questions to survey each other. For an added creative constraint, the teacher can give them specific grammar points to work with. For example, the teacher may want students to practice the present perfect, yet questions such as "Have you ever hit your partner?" are too personal, and would naturally elicit a "no" response. However, it is possible for students to come up with cleverly worded questions such as "If you know your brother has hit his girlfriend, would you tell her to leave him?"

The students walk around the room and survey their classmates. Each partner can interview half of their classmates. They need to make sure to keep the results secret.

THE GAME

Students play in two teams. The teams flip a coin to decide who goes first. The teacher chooses one of the questions the students have written and reads it aloud. The team gives their answer and wins the point if they are correct. Then it's team B's turn, and so forth.

Follow-up tasks

Speaking: The class can discuss what they think about healthy and unhealthy relationships.

Writing: Students write a pamphlet on the dangers and symptoms of abusive romantic relationships. They can distribute these around the school or other places where they study.

GAME 28

THE UN-AMERICAN DREAM

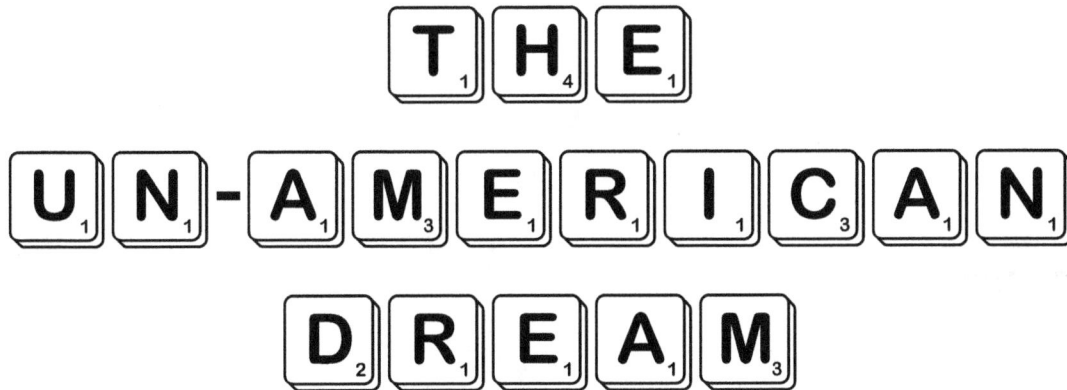

Why play the game

Nineteenth-century American writer and historian James Truslow Adams defined the "American Dream" in his book *The Epic of America* (1931) this way:

> Life should be better and richer and fuller for everyone, with opportunity for each according to ability or achievement regardless of social class or circumstances of birth.

This means that many want to believe that the United States is a place where anyone who works hard can achieve success. Unfortunately, this is not always true. There is still a great deal of inequality in the United States (as, indeed, in every country on Earth!). Those who are born white, Christian and male, particularly those from middle or upper-class families are privileged, and have opportunities that are often (though not always) unavailable to people from other backgrounds.

If your students have watched movies or read books with realistic characters, they can talk about the different characters in the stories and compare the obstacles they have faced in trying to achieve their dreams.

Game objective

To see what social obstacles lie in the way of achieving dreams

End point of the game

The player who achieves the highest score wins

Type of game

Dice

Number of players

5 to 10

Level/age of players

Teenagers and older, advanced and higher

Preparation time

None

Playing time

10-30 minutes

Materials and space required

Dice, a table and enough seats for every player

Instructions

Before the game: Students will have read several great works of fiction or watched movies made from these works, either on their own or as part of a curriculum. They may have read these works in their language arts classes in their native language. (For example, nearly everyone has learned about *Romeo and Juliet*.) The game works better if students have been exposed to American literature, particularly that which is written by women, minorities, and people of color in the United States. A partial list of such works, many of which have been made into excellent movies, includes:

- *The Color Purple*, by Alice Walker
- *To Kill a Mockingbird*, by Harper Lee
- *The Chosen*, by Chaim Potok
- *Flowers for Algernon*, by Daniel Keyes
- *The Joy Luck Club*, by Amy Tan
- *The Crucible*, by Arthur Miller
- *Breakfast at Tiffany's*, by Truman Capote
- *Lakota Woman*, by Mary Crow Dog (non-fiction)
- *The Autobiography of Malcolm X*, by Malcolm X and Alex Haley (non-fiction)
- *The Divine Secrets of the Ya-Ya Sisterhood*, by Rebecca Wells
- *A Raisin in the Sun*, by Lorraine Hansberry (a play)

Players take turns to name a character in a book, play, or movie such as one from the list above, and consider the following "strikes" that people may have against them when achieving their dreams:

- Gender (it is easier to achieve financial success as a male)
- Ethnicity (it is easier to achieve financial success as Caucasian)
- Money (it is easier to achieve financial success if if someone is born wealthy)
- Family (it is easier to achieve financial success if one's family can provide emotional, social, and financial support)
- Ability (it is easier to achieve financial success if ones has had a good education, or is able-bodied)
- Values/beliefs (it is easier to achieve financial success if one's values/beliefs match those of the majority group)

THE GAME

Players roll the dice and try to name a living American (or person known in the local culture) who has achieved financial success despite having the same number of "strikes" against them as the number shown on the dice.

Follow-up tasks

Speaking: Students brainstorm and analyze all of the ways in which they, as a group might be disadvantaged in their country. Then, they brainstorm and analyze all of the ways that they, as a group, enjoy privileges that others in their country may not.

Writing: Students research and write essays on whether or not they believe in the American Dream, or the idea that hard work will result in success. They should provide clear examples and arguments to support their statements.

GAME 29

U N D O C U M E N T E D

Why play the game

Undocumented immigrants often cannot attend school, go to a hospital, get a job, or purchase a car or a house.

Game objective

To understand the obstacles faced by undocumented immigrants

End point of the game

The player who gets to the end of the board first is the winner

Type of game

Board game

Number of players

2 to 6

Level/age of players

Teenagers and older, intermediate and higher

Preparation time

5 minutes to print the board

Playing time

10 to 15 minutes

Materials and space required

Table and chairs, tokens, a coin

Instructions

Before the game: Students consider what privileges citizenship confers on a person in a country.

T₁H₄E₁ G₂A₁M₃E₁

Players flip coins (head = 1 space, tails = 2 spaces) to move their token along the spaces on the board, but if they land on a square marked with something they cannot do, they are "deported" from the game (downloadable/photocopiable version found at http://wayz-goosepress.com/wp-content/uploads/2016/09/Social-Change-Game-29.pdf).

HOSPITAL		HOSPITAL	
	UNIVERSITY		CAR
HOUSE		UNIVERSITY	
CAR			JOB
	SCHOOL	JOB	
JOB			SCHOOL
	HOSPITAL	SCHOOL	
player 1	player 2	player 3	player 4

Follow-up tasks

Speaking: The students can debate how much the receiving country should do for illegal immigrants and what rights these immigrants and their children should be entitled to.

Writing: Students write an essay on the advantages and disadvantages of accepting immigrants into a country. They should start by explaining which type of immigrant they are referring to. For example, are the immigrants highly educated or not? Are they talking about immigrants who have left their country by choice or as refugees? Are they writing about immigrants who want to come to the country to join their family or are they coming for a job? Then they should write about the pros and cons of accepting particular types of immigrants. They should provide clear examples and arguments to support their statements.

GAME 30

FINAL CHALLENGE

Why play the game

Most religions and cultures believe in peace and non-violence. Some cultures take this idea to include animals and nature. For this reason, some believe in vegetarianism, and others have sacred rituals involving the natural world.

Many people further believe that the philosophy of non-violence applies not only to actions but also to thoughts and feelings. For example, saying or thinking un-kind things about someone is considered an act of violence against that person.

Game objective

To practice non-violence

End point of the game

Learning to live in a spirit of non-violence is the end point of the game. However, we are human and we make mistakes. Non-violence includes forgiving ourselves for these mistakes and promising to do better. Therefore, the end point of the game is for each player to go ever longer periods of time living the philosophy of non-violence.

Type of game

Challenge over time

Number of players

Unlimited

Level/age of players

All ages, all levels

Preparation time

None

Playing time

As long as possible

Materials and space

None required

Instructions

Before the game: The students discuss the idea of non-violence outlined above.

T H E   G A M E

Each player writes a definition of non-violence that they, individually, feel comfortable with. For example, many people may not wish to become vegetarian, but many will want to make a conscious effort to stop speaking negatively about people or gossiping.

Each player writes a pledge to live for as long as possible with this definition. They sign the pledge and begin the challenge.

Follow-up tasks

Speaking: Students can do research on how people in different cultures try to practice non-violence. For example:

- The Jewish people observe *Shabbat*, a day on which they attempt to appreciate the world God has given them without changing it in any way. They do not cook, clean, write, drive, or carry money from sundown on Friday nights to one hour after sundown on Saturdays.
- The Jains, Hindus and Buddhists practice what they call *ahimsa*, which is non-violence to all living beings. They believe in the concept of *karma*, which states that to hurt any living being is to hurt oneself, as we all have the same spark of divine energy.
- People of Christian faiths such as Catholics, Protestants, Mormons, and others are all followers of the teachings of Jesus Christ. These include the idea of "turning the other cheek" which means forgiving others and avoiding taking revenge.
- The word *Islam* comes from the word *salam* meaning "peace" (*Muslim Voices*, 2016). *Jihad*, often translated as "holy war", actually means "to struggle" (Islamic Supreme Council, 2016). The idea is that people of the Islamic faith believe in the struggle to find peace, both in their communities and within themselves.
- Many Native American cultures and African tribes, as well as Aborigines in Australia, believe that living harmony with nature, animals and other people is the only way to be truly happy.
- Students then present their findings to each other to encourage discussion.

Writing: Students keep a daily journal of their attempts to practice non-violence. The teacher may review these to check that they are being completed, but the student should be permitted to keep the contents private if they so desire.

BIBLIOGRAPHY

Bogost, I. (2007). *Persuasive games: The expressive power of video games.* Cambridge, MA: MIT press.

Costikyan, G. (1994). I have no words and I must design. *Interactive digra.org/ wp-content/uploads/digital-library/05164.51146.pdf*

Duflo, E., & Banerjee, A. (2011). *Poor economics: A radical rethinking of the way to fight global poverty.* New York: PublicAffairs.

Garfield, R. (2000). Metagames. In J. E. Dietz (ed.), *Horsemen of the Apocalypse: Essays on roleplaying* (pp. 16-22). Charleston, SC: Jolly Roger Games.

Gee, J. (2003). *What video games have to teach us about learning and literacy.* New York: Palgrave/Macmillan.

Islamic Supreme Council. (2016, 07/14). islamicsupremecouncil.org/ understandingislam/legal-rulings/5-jihad-a-misunderstood-concept-from-islam.html

Jacobs, H. A. (1861). *From incidents in the life of a slave girl* . Boston: Dover Thrift Editions.

Kenner, R. (Director). (2008). *Food, Inc.* [Motion Picture].

McGonigal, J. (2012). *Reality is broken: Why games make us better and how they can change the world.* New York: Penguin Press.

Muslim Voices. (2016, 07/14). muslimvoices.org/word-islam-meaning/

Packard, E. (1979-1998). *Choose your own adventure (series).* New York: Bantam Books.

Pollan, M. (2016). *The omnivore's dilemma: A natural history of four meals.* New York: Penguin Press.

Salen, K., & Zimmerman, E. (2004). *Rules of play: Game design fundamentals.* Cambridge, MA: MIT Press.

Schell, J. (2015). *The Art of Game Design: A Book of Lenses.* Pittsburgh, Pennsylvania: CRC Press.

Suits, B. (1978). *The grasshopper: Games, life and Utopia.* Toronto: University of Toronto Press.

The best of global digital marketing. (2016, 07/12). best-marketing.eu/case-study-metro-trains-dumb-ways-to-die/

About the Author

Janine Berger grew up in Canada and has taught English in Asia, the Middle East, and in Central and South America. She currently teaches English and trains English teachers at Universidad de los Hemisferios in Quito, Ecuador. She believes the interactive participation in games is the best way to motivate students to learn.

Follow Janine Berger on Facebook at janine.berger.5492 and Twitter as @teacherjanine.

～

Thank you for your time and attention! If you found the book useful, we hope you will leave a short review on the site where you purchased this book to let other readers know of your experience.

To be notified about new titles and special contests, events, and sales from Wayzgoose Press, please visit our website at wayzgoosepress.com or sign up for our mailing list by going to eepurl. com/bSGudb. (We send email infrequently, and you can unsubscribe at any time.)

～

9 781938 757280